Straight Talk About Eating Disorders

Straight Talk About Eating Disorders

Michael Maloney, M.D., and Rachel Kranz

☑® Facts On File, Inc.

Straight Talk About Eating Disorders

Copyright © 1991 by Elizabeth A. Ryan

All rights reserved. No part of this book may be reproduced or utilized in any form or by any means, electronic or mechanical, including photocopying, recording, or by any information storage or retrieval systems, without permission in writing from the publisher. For information contact:

Facts On File, Inc.
11 Penn Plaza
New York NY 10001

Library of Congress Cataloging-in-Publication Data
Maloney, Michael, 1944–
    Straight talk about eating disorders / Michael Maloney and Rachel Kranz.
      p. cm.
    Includes index.
    Summary: Describes compulsive eating, bulimia, and anorexia and discusses the mixed messages given to women and girls about eating, weight, diet, and looks, and how these messages can be destructive.
    ISBN 0-8160-2414-6
    1. Eating disorders—Juvenile literature. 2. Compulsive eating—Juvenile literature. 3. Bulimia—Juvenile literature. 4. Anorexia nervosa—Juvenile literature. 5. Body image—Social aspects—United States—Juvenile literature. [1. Eating disorders. 2. Obesity. 3. Bulimia. 4. Anorexia nervosa.]
    I. Kranz, Rachel, II. Title.
RC552.E18M36   1991
616.85' 26—dc20   90-49707

Facts On File books are available at special discounts when purchased in bulk quantities for businesses, associations, institutions, or sales promotions. Please call our Special Sales Department in New York at 212/967-8800 or 800/322-8755.

You can find Facts On File on the World Wide Web at
http://www.factsonfile.com

Text design by Cathy Rincon
Cover design by Smart Graphics

Printed in the United States of America

This book is printed on acid-free paper

MP FOF 10 9 8 7 6 5 4

Contents

1. Mixed Messages:
   Society's Views on Food and Weight   1
2. Hunger, Weight, and Biology   20
3. When Food Is Your Best Friend:
   Compulsive Eating   27
4. The Disease of Self-Starvation:
   Anorexia Nervosa   47
5. The Binge-Purge Cycle: Bulimia   72
6. What Can I Do About It?:
   Getting Help   96
7. Where to Find Help   110

Index   119

The advice and suggestions given in this book are not meant to replace professional medical or psychiatric care. The reader is advised to consult his or her physician before undertaking any diet or excercise regimen. Readers should seek professional help if they suspect that they suffer from an eating disorder. The authors and publisher disclaim liability for any loss or risk, personal or otherwise, resulting, directly or indirectly, from the use, application, or interpretation of the contents of this book.

1

Mixed Messages: Society's Views on Food and Weight

Turn on any commercial television station or pick up any teen magazine, and what are you likely to see? You'll probably find at least one ad for some luscious food being eaten by happy, satisfied people. And you'll probably see many ads, articles, or programs featuring thin, glamorous models in tight designer jeans.

What's the message? Which is better—eating luscious food or being as thin as a model? What if dieting wears you out, leaving you tired, irritable, and feeling deprived? What if your body doesn't get model-thin, no matter how much you diet? Can eating delicious food really make you happy? How do you figure out the ways of eating and the ways of looking that are right for you?

These aren't easy questions in our society. Girls especially get a lot of mixed messages when it comes to food, dieting, and body shape. On the one hand, a girl is supposed to be a good cook. She's supposed to be sociable and go places with her friends, including out to eat.

On the other hand, girls—and boys—are surrounded by extremely unrealistic pictures of thin women, women whose diets and natural body shapes will never be possible for the vast majority of women. Even if you're at the weight that is perfect for you, it's easy to feel like a failure if you're comparing yourself to a movie star or to *Seventeen*'s cover girl.

This problem of girls and women comparing themselves to "ideal women" has gotten more difficult in recent years. A look at the measurements of *Playboy* centerfolds and Miss America finalists over the past 20 years shows that, although these women who to many symbolize beauty have been getting slightly taller, they have also been weighing less and less. In other words, society's ideal woman has been getting thinner and thinner—and much more difficult for most people to imitate.

Of course, most women have never looked like their society's great beauties. But today's standards of feminine thinness are more unrealistic than they have ever been. By today's standards, even the beautiful 1950s movie star Marilyn Monroe would be considered overweight.

Most of us learn to live with these conflicting pressures. Once in a while, we may pig out when we're feeling low or when we're out with our friends. And we may spend more time than we'd like worrying about diets, weight, and the size of our jeans. But painful as these thoughts might sometimes be, they're only a part of our lives. Girlfriends, boyfriends, school, work, sports, our families, our hopes, dreams, and plans for after school are far more important in our lives than what we eat and how much we weigh. For some of us, however, these thoughts of and worry about food, weight, and diet become more important than anything else. These people suffer from *eating disorders*.

What Is an Eating Disorder?

A person has an eating disorder when she uses food to work out her emotional problems. Instead of feeling upset about a difficult situation, a person with an eating disorder tries to get rid of her feelings by eating or by dieting. In a sense, someone with an eating disorder is addicted to food or to dieting, rather like an alcoholic is addicted to liquor or a drug addict to drugs. Instead of food being one part of her life, it becomes her whole life.

A person with an eating disorder may eat huge amounts of food even when she's not hungry. She may even eat food that she doesn't like, just because she feels she has to eat. That's called *compulsive eating*.

Or a person may diet to the point of being down to 85% of her normal body weight, literally starving herself to death. That's called *anorexia nervosa*.

Finally, a person with an eating disorder may *binge*—eat huge amounts of food in a very short time—and then *purge*—vomit or use laxatives—in order to get rid of what she's just eaten. That's called *bulimia*.

On the surface, these eating disorders may seem very different from one another. But they all have one thing in common. If you suffer from them, you are constantly preoccupied with food, weight, and dieting. Friends, family, and schoolwork become less and less important. A good day isn't when your team wins the game or when you and a friend have a great talk—it's when you stuck to your diet or when the scale read what you wanted it to read. A bad day is when you ate something you weren't "supposed to" or when the number on the scale was too high—no matter what other good things might have happened. Food, weight, and dieting become ways to avoid all the other issues of your life.

Because food and dieting are such difficult topics, it's not always easy to tell the difference between an eating disorder and a normal amount of thinking about weight. As you read the specific chapters of this book, you'll get a clearer idea of what kind of behavior is part of each eating disorder and how to tell it from behavior that is not disordered. In general, however, an eating pattern becomes a disorder when it starts to interfere with another aspect of a person's life.

For example, a girl may spend a good deal of time thinking about her weight and how she looks. If she refuses to go to a party because she's "too fat," however, she may be beginning a pattern that may result in an eating disorder. How much you weigh should not be ruling your decisions about your social life.

Of course, if you find yourself allowing this to happen only once or twice, it may be painful, but it's probably not an eating disorder. We all have good days and bad days, for many different reasons. But if missing social activities because of weight becomes a pattern, it may very well indicate the beginning of a disorder. In that case, the person is saying that her friends, her social life, and her activities are less important to her than how much she weighs.

Likewise, if a person likes to have a sundae or a piece of pizza when she's feeling low, that's not necessarily an eating disorder. But if someone feels that the only thing she can really count on to make her happy is food, that is a problem.

Why is it important to identify eating disorders, and to tell them from normal eating patterns? The reason is not to label someone, but rather to understand what kind of problem the person is dealing with. If someone is a compulsive eater, an anorexic, or a bulimic, she will probably not be able to solve her problem by herself, using simple willpower or a new diet. The problem isn't lack of willpower—it's that the person is unwilling to face certain difficult feelings and is using food to help her avoid them. That problem will only be resolved when the person can face the hidden emotions and deal with them directly, rather than through food.

Eating Disorders and Teenage Girls

You may have noticed that this book has been using the word *she* to refer to people with eating disorders. That's because most people with eating disorders are girls or women. Only about 5% of all people with anorexia are male. The figure is roughly the same for bulimia. There is a somewhat higher figure for male compulsive eaters, but even so, most people with that disorder are female.

There are several reasons why women suffer from eating disorders far more than men. For one thing, society has not placed such a great emphasis on how much men weigh. Of course, a man is not supposed to be *obese* (extremely fat, at least 25% over your ideal body weight as determined by a doctor). But the acceptable range for men's weights is much greater than for women's. Magazines directed at men and boys rarely contain information about diets, suggestions for losing weight, or tips on clothes that will make them look slimmer. Men in professions where their weight is important—dancers, jockeys, and models—tend to have a higher rate of eating disorders.

Another reason why girls and women suffer from eating disorders has to do with anger and aggression. In our society, girls have traditionally been encouraged to be sweet and agreeable. Many girls feel they are not supposed to get angry, raise their voices, or aggressively go after something that they want. Many families teach their daughters to keep smiling, even if they are upset. They tell girls to think of others first, not themselves, even if it means losing a game or doing without something they want.

Girls who don't feel free to express their angry or aggressive feelings may decide to channel those feelings into an obsessive desire to control their weight. Controlling their bodies provides them with the illusion that they are controlling "bad" feelings. This is especially true of girls who are getting mixed messages: on the one hand, think of other people first; on the other hand, get good grades, do well in sports, or be successful. These girls may try to please their families on the outside—but inside, they would occasionally like to please themselves. Eating, dieting, or some combination of the two may appear to be safe ways of doing what *they* want to do, not what someone else wants them to do.

Of course, boys also have conflicts with their families and receive many troublesome mixed messages. However, because most people with eating disorders are not boys, it seems that most boys work out these problems in other ways, rather than through food and dieting. Therefore, in this book, we'll continue to use the word *she* when referring to someone with an eating disorder.

Food, Fights, and Families

In order to understand why some of us develop eating disorders, we have to look not just at our feelings about food, but at all of our feelings. After all, if eating disorders were only about food, they could be easily remedied by simple changes in diet. But eating disorders are more than a system of eating habits. They are a way of working out powerful feelings, feelings that the person with the disorder believes cannot be worked out any other way.

Many of these powerful feelings are rooted in the conflicts experienced by teenagers. The teen years are by definition a time of change. On the one hand, you are not yet an adult with your own home and your own income. Therefore, you don't have complete freedom to make all of your own decisions. And you probably still want your family's help in many areas, at least occasionally.

Your parents also expect you to need their help. At the very least, they probably feel responsible for feeding you and providing you with clothes, books, and school necessities. They probably also consider themselves responsible for giving you emotional, moral, and maybe academic guidance as well.

On the other hand, you are far closer to being an adult than you were a few years ago. Girls' bodies have begun to take on the adult qualities of *menstruation* (having your period), developing breasts, body hair, and hormonal changes. Teens of both sexes are probably aware of new sexual feelings, feelings that require you to make new kinds of decisions. You may already have a job or some other type of responsibility in your community. You are aware that soon, you will graduate from high school and be faced with a new set of adult decisions about work, school, and your future.

Your family may have various responses to your new condition. Some families recognize a teenager's growing maturity and accept it fairly easily. Even though they have their share of fights and misunderstandings, these families seem able to give teens the guidance they need while allowing them the freedom and responsibility that they are ready for. Both teenagers and adults in these families seem able to handle that difficult in-between time—no longer a child, not yet an adult.

Other families have a harder time with this transition. Some parents don't seem to realize that their teenagers are no longer children. They expect their offspring to need them just as much at age 15 as they did at age 8. These parents may have an especially difficult time recognizing that their daughters are becoming young women. They may prefer to think of a female child as "our little girl."

The daughter in such a family faces a number of conflicting pressures. She wants to try out her growing independence—but her family is telling her that she isn't ready to do so. If she believes them, she feels frustrated and deprived: why isn't she ready to go out on dates, pick out some of her own clothes, and make some of her own school decisions? What's wrong with her? But if she doesn't believe her family, she may feel even more conflicted: if she disagrees, does this mean that her family won't love her any more? If she chooses to be more independent, is she also choosing to be isolated and abandoned?

A daughter in such a family may feel guilty for wanting to be more independent and adult. If her parents feel threatened or distressed at "losing their little baby," she may feel that she doesn't have the right to cause them pain.

At the same time, she can't just turn off her wishes for more independence. Like all teenagers, she wants the right to explore new ideas, new abilities, and new relationships. How will she manage the conflict between her own wishes and those of her family?

Many girls in such families develop eating disorders. These girls feel that the one area of their lives that they can control is their own bodies. If they are compulsive eaters, they may feel that food is their substitute for the independence they are not allowed to have. They may also use food and fat to cover up their anger with their parents, anger that they don't feel comfortable expressing openly.

Anorexics or bulimics in such families may feel that the "secret" nature of anorexia and bulimia helps give them "secret" independence—a way to pursue their own goals without disturbing their parents. Anorexics often diet secretly—pushing food around on their plates to make it look like they're eating, or eating a normal meal and then using laxatives or vomiting to "get rid of" the weight. In fact, many families do not recognize the weight loss of the anorexic until it has become a serious medical problem.

Likewise, bulimics often binge and purge in secret. Unlike anorexics, they are usually of average weight, so it may be even easier for them to keep their secret. To teens in families that are unwilling to accept their independence, secret eating, dieting, and purging may seem literally like a way to "have their cake and eat it, too"—to do what they want without disturbing their families.

Other families may recognize that a teenager is becoming an adult—and increase their demands. Some families seem to expect perfection from their teenage daughters. They expect their children to perform well in school, sports, and extracurricular activities, with an eye constantly on their futures in college and afterward. Such families have probably always had unrealistically high standards, but as children become teenagers and can in fact do more, the family's demands intensify.

Other families may increase their demands on a teen's household responsibilities. Or, more subtly, they may increase their emotional demands, expecting teenage children to act like parents. Sometimes the teenager is expected to act as a parent to younger brothers and sisters. Other times, the teen is expected to act as a parent to an adult—to put the adult's needs first at all times, to care for the adult, and to view the adult as helpless, needy, or out of control.

This takes place in all types of families, but is especially common in single-parent families where the oldest girl may be "Mommy's best friend" or "Daddy's little wife and mother." Likewise, families where a parent has a drug or alcohol problem may expect a teenage daughter to become a "little mother" and help make up for the problem parent.

Teenagers in families like these may also develop eating disorders. The teenager who feels that she's expected to put her mother's feelings ahead of her own may well feel that the one comfort she can give herself is food. The teenager who feels burdened with emotional or financial responsibilities that she's not ready for may want to put a layer of fat between herself and the world, a buffer to protect herself from needs that she can't meet or demands she can't handle. These kinds of responses could lead a teenager to become a compulsive eater.

Because in our society fat bodies are not considered perfect, the compulsive eater may also be using her body size as a hidden way to rebel. On the surface, she is trying to meet her family's high standards for her. Meanwhile, though, her body is saying, "I can't always be perfect—you have to recognize that." If the teen doesn't feel comfortable confronting her family directly, she may feel compelled to do so indirectly, through her appearance.

Teens who feel that their parents expect them to achieve perfection in all areas may respond by developing anorexia or bulimia. Anorexics often stop menstruating because their bodies are trying to conserve all the nourishment they can, unwilling to release any of it in menstrual blood. Anorexics may also starve away signs of growing womanhood—breasts, hips, and womanly curves. The anorexic who feels pressured by her family's growing demands may be using her body to say, "Hey, look, I'm still a little girl." This may also be a hidden way to reassure the overprotective family we saw above.

Girls may also develop bulimia as a response to family pressures. If a girl feels that her family expects her to do everything well or to meet demands that she finds overwhelming, the girl may try to live up to these expectations but feel continually unable to do so. However, if her family seems to be loving and supportive, the girl may not know how to express the discomfort she feels. If she told her parents directly, "I can't do everything you think I can," they would probably not accept it. They might say, "Oh, sure you can, you just don't realize how great you are," which only adds to the pressure. Or they might say, "But we love you no matter what you do," which the girl senses is not completely true—she has felt their disappointment when she gets a "B" or comes in second at track, no matter how much they try to deny it.

Bulimia may be such a girl's way to manage her own anxieties. She is not "supposed" to feel nervous, worried, or pressured—after all, she should just remember how "great" she is. She is not "supposed" to be angry with her parents' demands—after all, they will love her no matter what. What does she do, then, if she *does* feel angry and pressured? She may work out these "unacceptable" feelings through bingeing and purging. This allows the girl to hide her true anger, frustration, and feelings of inadequacy from her parents—and from herself.

Perhaps the best way to sum up the relationship between food and families is to say that all families have rules, whether or not these rules are spoken. If these rules aren't working, sometimes people develop eating disorders in response.

A spoken family rule might be, "You must be home by 10 P.M. on school nights." An unspoken family rule might be, "When you meet a disappointment, don't let it bother you. Instead, act cheerful and ready to take on the next challenge."

The problem with these unspoken rules is that sometimes they don't work. And when rules are unspoken, it's very difficult to realize that they don't work or to do anything about them. If you feel very disappointed but are not "supposed" to be bothered, a rule that says "don't be bothered" does not make sense. But because this rule is unspoken, it may be hard to identify. You may only know about this rule because of how your parents have acted. Perhaps one day you came home crying and disappointed, and they seemed to be disappointed in *you*. When you cheered up, so did they. So you got the message that you were not supposed to be disappointed because your parents didn't like it.

If you can talk about an unspoken rule, you may be able to change it. You might say, "Hey, when I'm sad and disappointed, of course I'll show it, and I'd like a little sympathy instead of someone telling me not to feel so bad." If you can put these feelings into words, you might feel better even if your family's behavior doesn't change.

But when someone has trouble with her family's rules, spoken or unspoken, and feels that she cannot change them openly, then she will probably try to fight for change in a hidden way. An eating disorder may be one way of doing that—one way of showing that your family's rules are not working for you without your having to come right out and say it. That's why an eating disorder can't be controlled without being understood. Trying to fight it just means you are pushing down feelings that have already been pushed down. This only makes your feelings more stubborn—they've been disregarded once already, and they're not going to go away.

Anger and Appetite

One of the most common unspoken rules in families where there are eating disorders is "Don't be angry. And if you are angry, don't show it." Girls especially get the message that they are never supposed to get angry—and particularly not with their mothers or fathers or with anyone else who is supposed to love them.

The problem with this rule is that it's impossible to keep. Everyone gets angry sometimes, and we all get particularly angry with the people we love. We especially tend to get angry with our parents because as children we depend on them and so we are even more upset and disappointed if they don't act the way we'd like them to.

The teen years also tend to be a particularly angry time. Some of these stormy feelings are caused by hormonal changes, which may contribute to irrational or intense feelings. Being a teenager may also be frustrating because it is a time of change. Because you and your abilities are changing so fast, it isn't clear how much freedom, independence, and responsibility you can handle, or when you want to lean on someone older and more experienced. Not knowing exactly what you want or need from day to day may make you angry—with your family and with yourself.

Because teenagers are changing physically as well as in other ways, many people are very sensitive about their appearance at this time. If your family has unspoken rules that allow some people to comment on how you look, or allow certain kinds of comments to be made, this can be a frightening, upsetting, or angering experience.

For all of these reasons, it's natural for teens to feel angry at least some of the time and, particularly, to feel angry with their families. But if a girl believes that these feelings make her a bad person or will lead her family to stop loving her as a result, she may need to find a hidden way of expressing them. Developing an eating disorder may be a way of dealing with angry feelings that a girl is afraid to express in any other way.

Another unspoken family rule common in eating-disorder families is "Don't need too much" or "If you get a lot of something, that means someone else isn't getting enough." Children in these families may feel that they are too demanding, too greedy, or too selfish. Or they may be continually afraid of developing those qualities and may be willing to go to great lengths to prove to others and themselves that they are really very self-sufficient and unselfish.

This type of family often has parents who themselves are very needy and insecure. Even though such parents may seem to be strong and self-confident, they actually require a great deal of reassurance, even from their children. Such parents may worry, for example, when a child gets a poor grade or has a fight with a friend, fearing that this means that they, the parents, have somehow failed. Instead of getting comfort and assistance from her parents, the child has to make sure that *they* feel OK about *her* problem. The child in such a family becomes more concerned with meeting her parents' needs than with meeting her own.

Likewise, in families where one or both parents have a drug or alcohol problem, the child gets the message that she cannot depend on anyone else to take care of her. Even if one parent does not drink or take drugs, that parent may be more concerned with the problem parent than with the child, who is expected to put her own needs aside and to fend for herself.

No child likes to admit that she can't depend on her parents. After all, when you're only three or five or eight years old, you're in big trouble if there's no adult to take care of you. So children in such families do everything they can to hide their feelings of fear and anger. They do their best to go along with their parents' message: my needs come first, and yours come last.

But, as we've seen, feelings don't really go away when you hide them—they just come out in another way. Children who aren't allowed to express their own needs may decide that eating disorders are a safe way to do so. A child who must depend on herself may feel that feeding herself is her one source of strength or comfort. A child who feels that she is not supposed to have needs may feel that by dieting to extremes, she can learn to control her needs and become strong and self-sufficient.

Of course, no one makes a conscious decision to develop an eating disorder. Many eating disorders are life-threatening, and all of them are bad for a person's health. Some people wonder if people with eating disorders really want to kill themselves or hurt themselves, because that is the result.

In fact, just the opposite is true. The person with an eating disorder feels that eating or dieting in the disordered way is the only way she can protect herself. Whatever she knows consciously, unconsciously she feels that she *must* eat or starve herself or binge and purge. She may be protecting herself from her "bad" anger, from the loss of her parents' love, from being left all alone with no one to take care of her, or from some other condition. Until she is willing to look at her real fears and her real feelings, her real angers and appetites, she will believe that the solution lies somewhere in her relationship to food.

Food and Sex

Teenage girls get lots of mixed messages about sex. As a teenage girl, you're supposed to be sexy, good looking, and able to attract any boy you want. However you're not supposed to be too aggressive, come on too strong, or be too open about having sexual feelings.

On the one hand, you're supposed to spend lots of time making yourself look attractive—shopping, putting on makeup, exercising, dieting. On the other hand, you're not supposed to be too sure of yourself, or to act like all this hard work on your appearance entitles you to feel superior.

You're also not supposed to admit that you spend all of this time on your looks—especially not to boys. They're supposed to believe that your attractive appearance just happened naturally, not because you worked at it. They're supposed to believe that you aren't even aware of how good you look, not that you've been putting in a lot of time on yourself and want to see results in the form of their attention.

When you're actually having a relationship with a guy, the mixed messages don't stop. What if he seems very interested in sex or making out, and you don't share his feelings? What if you have strong sexual feelings—but don't want the same kind of physical relationship that the guy does? What if you do want exactly what he does—but worry that afterward, he'll think less of you? You don't want to be "frigid," but, you also don't want to be a "slut."

These mixed messages may come from your family, too. Your parents may want you to date and to be successful with boys—but they may also want you to stay "their little girl" and not develop any attachments that will take you away from them. Or your parents may say that they admire you, while making such "helpful" remarks as "Haven't you put on a few pounds, dear?" or "What makes you think you're old enough to wear a dress like that?"

However supportive your parents may seem, you may sense that your mother feels competitive with you, or that she's sad that you prefer going out on a date to staying home with her, the way you used to. You may have the impression that your father is nervous about your new woman's body, or that he is threatened by the attention that you are now getting from men.

Most teenagers experience at least some of these conflicts—in the world, with guys, and with their families. In families where the conflicts are especially intense, however, a teenage girl may try to resolve them by developing an eating disorder.

Again, no one makes a conscious decision to eat compulsively, to starve oneself, or to compulsively binge and purge. The person with the eating disorder may believe that she is acting in a sensible, rational way—eating food that she enjoys or preventing herself from putting on some unnecessary weight. Or she may sense that something is wrong but still feel that she has "no choice" but to eat or diet as she does. In either case, she is doing her best to handle some of the conflicts around sex and growing up—through her relationship to food.

The girl who eats compulsively may be trying to avoid sexual relationships altogether. She may believe that by being "too fat" to date, she can avoid having to make the painful choice between loyalty to her parents and having an independent relationship that disturbs them. Or, for the many heavy young women who do have satisfying sexual relationships, the fat may feel like a protection from parents' anger or from the world's disapproval of their own active sexuality.

Likewise, the anorexic may be literally trying to keep herself a "little girl" by starving away the signs of her growing adult sexuality: menstruation, breasts, and womanly curves. She may also be trying to give herself the thin, hard body of a man or boy, rather than what she sees as the soft, "fat" body of a woman.

The bulimic looks normal in appearance, so her eating disorder doesn't affect her relationships in the same way. But her ritual of stuffing herself and then vomiting or using a laxative may be a way of acting out her conflicting feelings about her sexuality—that it's both something she "can't get enough of" and something that she'd like to get rid of. She might also be expressing the idea that while on the surface she looks normal, inside, she has a hidden, ugly secret—her sexuality.

Some girls have even more difficult conflicts about sex. They come from families where there is *incest* or *sexual abuse*; where children are not protected from the sexual attention of adults. Children in such families may actually be forced to have intercourse or some other physical contact with adults. Or they may be watched while getting undressed, taking a shower, or going to the bathroom; or put in the position of watching an adult perform these activities when they aren't comfortable with that. They may be subject to inappropriate remarks about their bodies or their sex lives. In all of these cases, the abuse means that an important boundary has been crossed.

Here, too, food may seem like a way to handle the conflict. Fat may feel like a buffer, a way of either making oneself unattractive or giving oneself strength—turning oneself into a big, powerful woman instead of a little girl who can't protect herself. The anorexic may be trying to keep herself a child who won't attract unwanted sexual attention that she isn't old enough to handle. The bulimic may be acting out the "ugly secret" of an incestuous relationship. (If you or someone you know is being sexually abused, we urge you to get help immediately in order to stop the abuse. Tell a sympathetic adult, call an incest hotline, or notify your local social service agency. You can find some hotline and agency numbers in Chapter 7 of this book.)

How to Use This Book

This book is your resource. In this chapter, we've given you an overview of eating disorders: what they are, how they relate to our society and our families, why people develop them. In the next chapter, we give you some basic information about the biology of hunger and weight: what happens in your body to make you feel hungry or full, how people gain weight, and what makes weight gain or weight loss vary.

The following three chapters provide a closer look at the three most common types of eating disorders: compulsive eating, anorexia, and bulimia.

In Chapter 6, we talk about getting help. We discuss why it may be difficult for someone with an eating disorder to seek help, what types of help are available, and what the benefits of seeking help might be. We also talk about how friends and family members may respond to a girl with an eating disorder—how they can be supportive and helpful while taking care of their own feelings concerning this difficult and painful subject.

The last chapter provides a list of resources—research centers, clinics, and support groups—for the person who is ready to seek help right now. It also provides phone numbers for hotlines that help with other problems often found in those with eating disorders, such as being a victim of sexual abuse, drug or alcohol abuse, or having a family member with a drug or alcohol problem.

If you or someone you know has an eating disorder, or if you suspect that this might be the case, you may want to turn right away to the chapter that best fits the situation. Or you may find it helpful to read all three chapters on eating disorders because they are often related. Many bulimics, for example, were once anorexics.

Then, when you've read about what the disorder is and how it works, we urge you to turn to Chapters 6 and 7 and find out about seeking help, for you or your friend. In either case, it's important to remember that the only one who can really seek help is the person with the disorder. Until she is ready to admit that she has a problem and is willing to address it, she won't be able to solve the problem.

The good news is that when a person *is* ready to seek help, the help is there. It is possible to change the patterns of compulsive eating, self-starvation, excessive dieting, bingeing and purging. It is possible to confront the feelings that led to the eating disorder and to resolve them in a different way, apart from food. It is possible to find the counseling and the support groups that are right for you or your friend and to put food back in its rightful place—as one small but enjoyable part of a rich, full life.

2

Hunger, Weight, and Biology

Sometimes we eat because we're hungry. But just about everyone eats for other reasons, as well. Likewise, sometimes we refuse food because we're not hungry. But most people also refuse food for other reasons: politeness, wishing to lose weight, embarrassment about being hungry, not wanting to be seen eating, or not wanting to eat when others are not eating.

These varied relationships make it difficult to decide when you are truly hungry and when you just feel like having something to eat. Perhaps some of the confusion can be cleared up if we begin with a biological explanation of what we know about hunger.

Scientists' theories about hunger are constantly changing, but currently we believe that hunger originates in the hypothalamus. The hypothalamus is the part of the brain that regulates body temperature, blood pressure, and heartbeat. It also regulates the body's blood-sugar level and the *metab-*

olism (processing) of fats and *carbohydrates* (starchy foods, such as bread, potatoes, and pasta).

These last two functions are the ones we're concerned with, for they help determine both hunger and body weight. Let's look at the blood-sugar level first.

Blood sugar is quite different from table sugar. When you eat nutritious food, the nutrients are converted into blood sugar, which is then further processed by *insulin,* a substance produced by an organ called the *pancreas.* Insulin helps to convert blood sugar into the materials that the body needs to grow and to restore itself. (Diabetics' bodies do not produce enough insulin, which is why they must take insulin supplements to process their blood sugar. Otherwise, no matter how much they might eat, their body would be unable to make use of the nutrition.)

Blood sugar can also be affected by foods that are not nutritious. Processed sugar, candy, cake, and other sweet things have a powerful effect on your body's blood sugar. So do alcohol, caffeine, nicotine, and many drugs.

The normal blood-sugar cycle works like this:

- Your blood sugar falls below a certain level. The hypothalamus registers this drop, and you experience a sensation of hunger.
- In response to the hunger, you eat something. The food you eat is converted into blood sugar.
- Your blood-sugar level goes up. You no longer feel hungry. This process usually takes about 20 minutes, which is why diet books tend to recommend a 20-minute wait between eating first and second helpings—it takes that long for your hunger to be affected by the food you ate.
- The rise in blood sugar triggers your pancreas to release insulin, which helps to convert the blood sugar into the materials your body needs.
- As the insulin processes your blood sugar, your blood-sugar level drops. Once again, you feel hungry.

As you can see, this whole process has little to do with whether your stomach is full or not. That feeling of being full is separate from the feeling of being satisfied—of having eaten enough nutrients to raise the level of your blood sugar.

Thus, if someone is used to eating huge quantities of food, stuffing herself until her stomach feels full, she might no longer recognize that other feeling of satisfaction, even though she may actually have gotten all the nutrients she needed. She might be looking for a different feeling that has nothing to do with what her body actually needs.

Many substances, however, can raise your blood-sugar level without actually being nutritious. Ironically, many of these substances have quite a dramatic effect on blood sugar, sending its level up in much less time than the 20 minutes required by other types of food.

For example, processed sugar and the foods that contain it send your blood sugar shooting up almost as soon as you swallow them. Alcoholic beverages are full of processed sugar, and they too make you feel less hungry while giving you a blood-sugar high.

Caffeine also acts very quickly on blood sugar, which explains some of the rush you get from drinking a cup of coffee and also explains why you might not feel hungry after drinking coffee, tea, caffeinated diet soda, or other non-calorie caffeinated beverages. Foods made with processed white flour also give you a quick fix of blood sugar.

The problem with all of these substances is that their high soon leads to a "crash." The quick infusion of sugar into the bloodstream triggers the pancreas to produce a larger than normal amount of insulin. (That's why diabetics aren't supposed to drink alcohol or eat sweet foods; their pancreases cannot produce extra insulin.) As you might expect, the extra-large dose of insulin processes a great deal of blood sugar very quickly—leading to a crash that produces still greater hunger than before.

You can see that a person who is used to eating a great deal, especially a great deal of sweet or starchy food, has developed a different relationship to hunger. She's not listening to the body signals that say "I've had enough nutrients—I'm satisfied." Instead, she's paying attention to how full her stomach feels. If she's used to eating sweet or starchy foods, she's probably looking for a quick rush. But soon after the rush, she always gets a crash, which can then only be satisfied by another quick rush.

Biology and Weight

We've described the biology of hunger. What about the biology of weight?

Once again, scientists have many different theories on this issue, and there is still a great deal of disagreement. There is also a great deal of false and incomplete information about weight gain that many people—and even some doctors—still believe.

One of the simplest theories of weight gain and loss is the calorie theory. In science, a *calorie* is a unit of heat. In nutrition, it's a way to measure the relationship between food and activity. A piece of food adds a certain number of calories to the body; a certain amount of activity burns up a certain number of calories. According to this theory, if a person takes in more calories than she burns up, she will gain weight; if she takes in fewer calories than she burns up, she will lose weight.

In fact, the body is somewhat more complicated than that. This is where metabolism—the body's processing of food—comes in.

Everyone has his or her own rate of metabolism. That's why some people can eat a great deal and not seem to gain weight, while others seem to gain weight even when they eat very little.

To some extent, metabolism rates run in families. However, because eating patterns and psychological relationships to food also run in families, it's hard to tell if heavy parents are passing on slow metabolisms to their heavy children or passing on certain habits and feelings about food—or both.

How food is metabolized plays an important role in how much weight gain it produces. For example, the liver plays an important role in metabolizing fat. A person with a weak liver—say, someone who has been drinking for several years—will have a more difficult time metabolizing fat than someone whose liver is in good condition. Thus alcoholics often gain a great deal of weight because of the difficulties they have in metabolizing fat. Ironically they may be suffering from *malnutrition*—a shortage of nutrients—even as they are gaining weight.

Some nutritionists attribute a great deal of weight gain to difficulties of the liver. They advocate a bland diet, low in animal fat and dairy products, and free of alcohol, sugar, caffeine, marijuana, and artificial ingredients, in order to ease the strain on the liver and allow that organ to metabolize fat more efficiently.

Another theory that deals with metabolism is the *set-point* theory. This way of thinking holds that we each have a set point—an equilibrium—where we are taking in just the right amount of food for the amount of activity we're involved in and are neither gaining nor losing weight. The body tries hard to maintain this equilibrium. In fact, the body tries particularly hard not to lose weight—a useful biological tendency from the days when food was scarce and weight loss might mean death.

Thus, according to this theory, dieting may actually cause a person to gain weight. Although the person is eating less food, the body doesn't "want" to lose weight. So the body responds to the new low food intake by dropping its metabolism and trying to "hold on" to all of its weight.

Discouraged with this response, the dieter may eventually break the diet. Then, although the diet has not helped the person lose any weight, the end of the diet may produce a gain in weight. Once the body is used to the new, lower metabolism, going back to its old eating habits feels like a big increase in food. This "increase" produces a new weight gain—even though the person is eating exactly the same foods as before she went on the diet.

Nutritionists and scientists have identified two ways to change a set point. The most reliable way is exercise. If your body is more active, it somehow recognizes that it needs more food, and its metabolism adjusts accordingly. At the new, higher metabolism, a person can eat more without gaining weight, or eat less and lose weight.

Some nutritionists also believe that the liver-friendly diet that we described before also helps change a person's metabolism. By not asking the liver to process sugar, fat, caffeine, alcohol, drugs, or preservatives, a person may be leaving it free to process food more efficiently. If metabolism works better, the result is a loss in weight. (This change may be confusing at first—producing a feeling of hunger and satisfaction at the same time as the body tries to adjust to this new metabolism.)

Finally, some scientists believe that our normal appetites are simply "set" too high. They believe that we are programmed to eat as though we were much more physically active than we are—as though we still depended on hard, physical labor to survive.

Coming to Terms With Your Hunger and Your Weight

If gaining or losing weight were a simple matter of biology, life would be much simpler for many of us. We could rationally choose a weight that was healthiest for us, and we would likewise choose the healthy diet and exercise plan that would naturally achieve that weight for us.

In fact, food, weight, and diets are highly charged emotional issues for almost everyone. Even those of us without eating disorders may be tempted to see eating sweets as "bad," following a diet as "being good," being thin as evidence of "strong will power," and being heavy as a kind of failure.

In the following three chapters, we'll take a closer look at the eating disorders that may arise from these close connections between food and emotional issues.

3

When Food Is Your Best Friend: Compulsive Eating

One of the challenges of understanding compulsive eating is that the definitions of hunger, appetite, and eating are so confused in our society. Of course, people must eat in order to survive, but people eat for many more reasons than that. How many of the following situations seem familiar to you, describing either your own eating habits or those of someone you know?

- A group of friends get together for a pleasant evening of talking and hanging out. They start by going out to dinner together, and later they go to a diner and have coffee and dessert.
- A girl and her mother are shopping in a mall. They spend all afternoon going from shoe store to shoe store, passing all of the mall's other stores, which include a caramel

corn stand, a candy store, an ice cream parlor, a coffee shop, and a cheese store. At the end of the day, they're exhausted, so they stop to have a snack.
- A couple on a date are watching a scary movie. Both the movie and the date are making them nervous. They feel calmer when they have something to do with their hands, so they each drink a giant coke and keep eating popcorn.
- A girl is working on a difficult paper for history. It's her worst subject, and she's scared that she's doing a terrible job. The paper is due tomorrow, and she knows she's going to be up all night. "When I get done with the next paragraph," she promises herself, "I get to have a snack."
- A guy goes to dinner at his girlfriend's house. His girlfriend's mother offers him some cabbage soup, saying, "It's my own special recipe." Even though he doesn't really like cabbage, he accepts the soup and even asks for seconds.
- A girl has just heard that her boyfriend was seen at a party with another girl—after he told her that he was too sick to keep their date. The girl is furious. She stalks into the kitchen and eats a big bowl of ice cream.

Do these scenes sound familiar? Besides eating to satisfy the body's hunger, people eat to be sociable, to celebrate, or just to have something to do. They eat out of nervousness, out of boredom, out of fear, out of anger, and out of the desire to please others. In our society, people are surrounded with constant opportunities to eat, even when they aren't hungry. It's no wonder that people get confused about their relationship to food.

Biological Factors in Compulsive Eating

As we saw in Chapter 2, feelings of hunger are related to blood-sugar levels. Nutritious food raises your blood sugar slowly, while sweet, starchy food raises it quite quickly, a sugar rush that is usually followed by a crash.

Thus the person who's used to eating sweet, starchy food is caught in a vicious cycle. The more gradual and long-lasting satisfaction of eating, say, a bowl of brown rice or a piece of fish, won't feel satisfying to someone who is looking for the dramatic rush of a piece of cake or a bowl of spaghetti. But that rush won't be satisfying for very long.

Part of the biological explanation for compulsive eating, then, has to do with getting used to certain reactions to food. The compulsive eater may have trained herself to look for these reactions—a very full stomach, a quick rush of blood sugar. Seeking these reactions practically guarantees that she will eat more food than her body needs while almost continually feeling hungry and unsatisfied.

Some people have a condition that further affects their relationship to hunger. That condition is known as *hypoglycemia*.

In a sense, hypoglycemia is the opposite condition from diabetes. Diabetics can't produce enough insulin to process their blood sugar. Hypoglycemics produce too much. As a result, their blood sugar is processed much more quickly than others', and it falls to unpleasantly low levels much more quickly as well. If hypoglycemics go for even a few hours without eating, they may react as drastically as if they had been starving for days: with intense hunger, confusion, memory loss, inability to concentrate, nervousness, anxiety, depression, a feeling of discouragement and despair, and possibly headache or other intense physical distress. Some hypoglycemics' condition is so severe that people actually black out or hallucinate from going without food.

To people who don't understand this condition, the hypoglycemic may seem like a person with no willpower or like someone who is being childish about food. When the hypoglycemic becomes nearly frantic from hunger, this may well be a genuine biological reaction—but people who don't understand the condition may easily think it's a psychological problem.

Ironically, hypoglycemics may crave sweet, starchy foods and caffeine, because they are looking for a quick fix to raise their blood-sugar level. But, as we've seen, these quick fixes produce quick crashes—crashes that are especially intense for hypoglycemics. If a person with hypoglycemia doesn't understand his or her condition, he or she may compulsively eat sweet, starchy foods to keep blood-sugar levels at a comfortable level, not realizing that these are the very foods that will soon produce the intense discomfort of a blood sugar crash.

The solution for hypoglycemics is to eat frequent, small portions of low-fat protein (fish, chicken, low-fat dairy products) and the so-called complex carbohydrates (whole grains like brown rice, oatmeal, and whole-wheat bread). They should generally avoid sweet, starchy foods, alcohol, and caffeine, particularly on an empty stomach.

If you think you might be hypoglycemic, you might work with a doctor or nutritionist to find the diet that is right for you. Or you might experiment yourself for a while: give yourself permission to eat as frequently as you like but eliminate foods with sugar, white flour, caffeine, and alcohol completely from your diet for at least two weeks. Pay attention to your feelings of hunger and what satisfies them when you don't have sugar and processed foods to fall back on. (When we say "sugar," we mean all sweeteners, including corn syrup, honey, barley malt, and molasses. Although artificial sweeteners do not trigger an insulin reaction in the same way, they tend to set off a craving for sweet things. Since that's what you're trying to avoid, you should probably avoid them too, if you want to give this experiment a fair shot.)

Even if you are not hypoglycemic, this experiment may give you some useful clues about your nutritional habits and needs. Some compulsive eaters may be suffering from nutritional deficiencies of a particular vitamin or mineral. They may eat compulsively, continually looking for the substance that will satisfy their craving.

To someone with a nutritional deficiency, sweet or starchy foods may seem like an attractive option because they seem to satisfy so quickly. However, because they have little or no nutritional value, very soon the person will be dissatisfied once again—and will return to eating compulsively.

Thus, it's possible to develop a kind of addiction to sugar or to a combination of sugar and caffeine. The body that is used to the quick blood-sugar fix from these foods will go into withdrawal without them, perhaps suffering from headaches, dizziness, or other intense physical discomfort. In such a state, it seems that only sugar or caffeine will satisfy the craving—but the satisfaction will soon turn into new cravings. The only solution is to quit cold turkey—to eliminate sugar and caffeine completely from your diet or at least to radically reduce the amount of it that you eat.

Chocolate, which contains both sugar and caffeine, is doubly addictive. People who feel like "chocaholics" may be considered low in willpower by others, but in fact, they're experiencing a powerful physical reaction. Again, the solution is to cut the substance that you crave out of your diet completely or to reduce it to the point where it no longer sets off the craving.

Of course, people who are prone to hypoglycemia face a double whammy from sugar, chocolate, caffeine, and processed flour. These substances tend to be addictive anyway; and their tendency to trigger the extra production of insulin and create a blood-sugar crash is especially powerful for hypoglycemics, who are prone to such crashes in any case.

It's interesting to note that many scientists see a link between the addictive power of sugar and that of alcohol, which is high in sugar. Some studies show that people who are prone to alcoholism are also prone to the compulsive eating of sweet, starchy foods. In addition to whatever psychological factors may be operating, such people's bodies may have become addicted to sugar.

Some people have allergies to other food substances that may affect their eating habits. These food allergies don't show themselves in the usual way—with coughing, sneezing, or hives. Instead, they produce the same type of crave-crash cycle as sugar or caffeine do. Allergies to wheat, to dairy products, and to some other foods often lead a person to crave huge amounts of the very food that his or her system cannot handle. Such cravings and allergies may be a factor in some compulsive eating. Work with a doctor or nutritionist can be useful in creating a diet that helps avoid such foods.

Recognizing Compulsive Eating

So far we've been talking about eating in purely biological terms. But, as we saw at the beginning of this chapter, people eat for many other reasons than to satisfy hunger. Even though compulsive eating may include some biological factors, it nearly always includes some psychological factors as well. A compulsive eater may well be trying to satisfy a craving for a lost nutrient or responding to a sugar crash, but she is almost certainly also working out some feelings through food rather than directly.

As we've seen, everyone needs food to live, and nearly everyone eats for reasons other than hunger, at least sometimes. So there is no hard and fast line between compulsive eaters and everyone else. In this section, we'll give various definitions and descriptions of compulsive eating, but there is no easy test that will definitely tell you whether someone is eating compulsively or not. If anything in this chapter rings a bell with you, either about yourself or about someone you know, it's likely that the person who comes to mind is a compulsive eater—someone who would benefit from some attention to the feelings that she is trying to work out through food.

One definition of a compulsive eater is someone whose days revolve around food. Her most intense emotions—fear, guilt, anticipation, pleasure—nearly all have to do with food—looking forward to a meal, feeling guilty for eating a sweet, being afraid that she is going to lose control and binge again. ("Bingeing" is eating large amounts of food in a very short period.) Other social events—family meals, times with friends, dates—are all seen in terms of food, whether the compulsive eater is looking forward to eating or being afraid that she will eat too much.

A compulsive eater keeps eating beyond the time when her hunger has been satisfied. Some compulsive eaters feel that once they start eating, they can't stop. They may feel stuffed or nauseated by the time that they do stop, but they continue to eat until they have finished a certain amount of food.

Others simply eat large or frequent portions of food. They eat in what seems a fairly "normal" way, but their eating is driven by anxiety, fear, frustration, or anger, rather than by hunger or even pleasure.

In general, compulsive eaters do not get a great deal of pleasure from food. Even those who think of food as their only comfort tend to feel a great deal of guilt and shame after they have eaten. They may be ashamed that they seem to have no other sources of pleasure, or they may feel guilty about eating and gaining weight. They may feel that their eating—and, if they are overweight, their weight—are evidence of a disgusting lack of self-control or proof that they can't properly manage their lives. They may also feel envious or inferior toward others who seem to handle food better, either because they eat less or because they seem to eat freely without gaining weight.

Other compulsive eaters get little pleasure out of food even when they are eating. Even while bingeing, they are not enjoying what they eat. They may binge on food that they normally don't like, such as cans of pork and beans, or cake mix out of the package. They may go from one restaurant to the next, eating an entire three-course meal at each one. They may eat entire pies and cakes, or gallons of ice cream, not savoring the taste, but simply taking in the food as quickly as possible.

A compulsive eater may also be a compulsive dieter. Some compulsive eaters stick rigidly to their diets. Although they may continue to control their urges to binge, they continually feel drawn to food in times of stress or anxiety, and the price they pay for their rigid self-control is the feeling that if they ever let go, they would be completely *out* of control.

Other compulsive eaters break their diets with occasional binges that are then followed by even more rigorous diets. Compulsive eaters of this type may be of average weight, but they are no less compulsive about food than the person who eats compulsively and is obese. Whether they are following or restraining their compulsions to eat, whether their compulsion results in a weight gain or not, they are still organizing their emotional lives around their feelings about food and weight.

Thus, both types of compulsive dieters regard food as an object of fear and anxiety, and both organize their thoughts and experiences around food.

The following are some other signs of compulsive eating. Remember that it's possible to be heavy or even obese and not to eat compulsively. It's also possible to be of average weight or even thin and to be a compulsive eater. What determines the problem is not the amount of weight (though this may be a clue in some cases) but the person's relationship to eating. If eating is genuinely a source of pleasure, if a huge meal is not followed by bouts of guilt and shame, if food is valued for its taste and nutrition and not for its ability to comfort, defuse anger, or calm a person down, then a person is not eating compulsively (though she may be eating unhealthily).

Possible Signs of Compulsive Eating:
- buying and eating food secretly
- being ashamed to be seen eating
- claiming to keep to a strict diet while remaining considerably overweight (a likely sign of secret eating)
- eating unusually huge quantities, such as entire cakes or pies, or more than one meal at a time
- eating continually, more frequently than three meals a day and an occasional snack
- frequently eating past the point of being physically full
- eating as the primary way to respond to bad news or good news
- eating while bored, nervous, frustrated, angry, or lonely
- planning one's days completely or primarily around eating or avoiding food
- having eating buddies—friends with whom most or all shared activities revolve around food
- having special rituals for food and eating
- being afraid to be left alone with food
- feeling a great deal of guilt and/or shame about food or eating
- alternating periods of heavy eating with periods of rigid dieting
- continual fear of being fat

Who Is a Compulsive Eater?

Although most compulsive eaters are women, the percentage is lower than for the other two eating disorders, anorexia nervosa and bulimia. Some 85% of compulsive eaters are women, as opposed to 95% and up for the other two disorders.

Compulsive eating may be found in people of all ages. As a learned response to emotional issues, it tends to run in families, although sometimes only one child will develop this eating disorder, possibly because he or she is closer to the parent who is also a compulsive eater.

Compulsive eating also cuts across class and cultural lines. However, different cultures have different attitudes about weight. Thus it may be more acceptable to eat more and to gain more weight in some cultures than in others. As we have seen, the amount that a person eats and the amount of weight she gains is not necessarily related to being a compulsive eater. Compulsive eating is determined not by the amount of food or weight, but by the way a person uses eating, food, and weight in her life.

Medical Effects of Compulsive Eating

Once a person is obese—at least 25% over her normal body weight as defined by a doctor—she does risk some physical problems. If she has gained weight through eating sweet foods, she may develop diabetes: through the years, eating all those sweets has required the pancreas to produce extra insulin, and finally, it just wears out. She may develop problems with her heart, her circulation, and her blood pressure, with increased tendency to heart attack and stroke. Some obese people develop problems with mobility and eventually become confined to wheelchairs.

However, most people who weigh more than they would like are not really risking any medical problems. And, as we've seen, they may be in greater danger from dieting and then regaining the weight than they are from keeping the weight on in the first place. Compulsive eating may lead to serious physical problems even when it doesn't lead to weight gain. Compulsive eating may become anorexia (self-starvation, see Chapter 4) or bulimia (bingeing and then purging, see Chapter 5), which present severe medical problems of their own.

Many studies have linked obesity to psychological problems, such as anxiety, depression, and low self-esteem. Here, too, the problem is complicated by society's attitudes: is obesity the result of these emotional difficulties, or do the difficulties come from society's negative attitudes towards heavy people? Sometimes, the fear of being fat itself may become an emotional problem, even in someone who is not actually heavy.

Likewise, sometimes weight *is* a sign of an inner emotional conflict. Sometimes it's the sign of a certain pattern of eating that may lead to weight gain, but isn't necessarily driven by emotional needs. And of course, given society's unrealistic attitudes about what girls should weigh, it's very difficult to determine whether you're "really" fat, a "little too" fat, or just the right weight for you, given that you'll probably never be as thin as a model.

Profiles of Compulsive Eaters

Following are three profiles of compulsive eaters. None of the people described here actually exist. Instead, these stories represent *composites*—combinations of various factors that are frequently found in the stories of compulsive eaters. Although these stories are not literally true, they will give you an accurate picture of the lives of many compulsive eaters.

Luisa, age 13, has always been known as a "fat kid." Everyone in her family—parents, aunts and uncles, and her five younger brothers and sisters—likes to tease Luisa about her weight. When Luisa gets annoyed, her parents tell her not to be so "sensitive." "Your family loves you, and teasing is one way to show it," her mother likes to say. "They wouldn't bother to make fun of you if they didn't care about you."

As the oldest child, Luisa has a lot of responsibilities at home. Both of her parents work, so Luisa is expected to come straight home from school every day and prepare the family meal while supervising her brothers and sisters. When Luisa asked if she could stay after for choir practice one day a week, her parents were shocked. "You know your sisters and brothers need you," her father said. "We all depend on you, Luisa."

Luisa knows that in her family, everyone has to help out at home. But she also has the feeling that her parents don't really want her to have friends outside the family. Both of them frequently make remarks like "You can't trust anyone like family," and "Blood is thicker than water." When Luisa was younger, she once brought a friend home and for the next week, her parents asked questions and made remarks: "So what does her father do?" "Is she a good student? You have to be careful not to hang around with bad students, Luisa, they'll get you in trouble." "How can her mother let her wear a dress like that? She must not care for her daughter at all!" Luisa got the message that her friends made her parents nervous.

Sometimes Luisa feels that the one thing in life that does make her happy is food. Every day on the way to school, she buys herself some candy bars, which she keeps hidden in her locker at school and in her bedroom at home. She daydreams about which stores she'll go to and which type of candy she'll buy. Then, after she's bought the day's supply of candy, she feels secure. Whenever something goes wrong, she can always think about that candy, waiting for her.

Luisa has a special way she likes to eat her candy. First she unwraps the entire candy bar, very carefully, without tearing the wrapper. Then she takes one slow bite, letting the candy melt in her mouth. She eats the rest of the candy bar very fast, filling up her whole mouth with the delicious taste and then swallowing as much as she can in one gulp.

Always a heavy kid, Luisa has been gaining a lot of weight in the past year. She feels that she is now so fat that everyone is always laughing at her. At school, she tries to avoid other kids as much as possible, so that no one will make fun of her. Even if someone is nice to her, Luisa tries to slip away because she's sure that the person is only being nice in order to get the chance to make fun of her later.

As far as dating, Luisa doesn't even think about going out with anyone. First of all, she knows her parents—who are quite religious—would not approve. Second, she's sure that nobody would ever find her attractive—she's way too fat.

Maggie, age 15, was of average weight as a child. But ever since her parents got divorced, she has been gaining weight. At first, Maggie lived with her mother, but the two of them had never gotten along well. So when Maggie's father remarried, she asked to live with him. Maggie's stepmother wasn't very enthusiastic at first, but finally agreed that Maggie could stay with them during the school year if she went back to her mother for the summer.

Maggie has lots of close friends, and she's very popular with guys. She's had a steady boyfriend and two or three close girlfriends since she was 13, with lots more boys and girls eager to be her friend or her boyfriend whenever she wants. Although Maggie gained about 20 pounds in the first two months that she lived with her father, her boyfriend is still crazy about her and a couple of other guys in her class have let her know that they would be happy to date her whenever she wants.

Maggie's father and stepmother have noticed Maggie's weight gain, but they figure that she's just upset about the divorce and is bound to lose the weight soon. Maggie herself isn't quite sure how the weight gain happened. She doesn't seem to be eating any differently than usually—she's just found herself eating *more*.

Sometimes Maggie does try to diet. She promises herself to have only one helping of everything and to cut out dessert. But somehow, when the food is right there in front of her, she can never stick to her resolution. She just continues to have seconds, and sometimes thirds, and to eat one or two desserts at every meal. She doesn't even notice she's doing it until after the meal is over. Then she feels bad and makes another promise—but she's beginning to think she can't trust herself to do *anything* the way she plans.

Charisse is 17. She's tall and thin, and many other girls at her school envy her great figure. They also envy Charisse's incredible self-control, for she seems to be always on a diet and not to care about food at all.

Charisse's parents are very proud of her, and they expect a lot from their daughter. When Charisse comes home with good grades, they celebrate by buying her a special present, but when when she brings home a B or even an A-minus, her father demands an explanation. Charisse thinks of her father as very fair—if she can come up with a good explanation and a sincere promise to do better, he will accept it. But she can tell he's disappointed, all the same.

Lots of boys want to go out with the attractive and popular Charisse, but she's not really interested in a steady boyfriend. She has some friends that she hangs out with sometimes, but she's not really close to anyone. Somehow it never quite "clicks" with anyone to be a really close boyfriend or girlfriend.

Charisse also has a secret that she would never tell anybody. Sometimes she binges—she eats huge amounts of food without being able to control herself. Because the rest of the time Charisse is on a strict diet, she doesn't ever gain weight, but she is always afraid she is going to.

Charisse doesn't even like the things she eats when she gets out of control. Sometimes she eats boxes of cake mix, straight from the package, or jars of peanut butter, or whole cartons of sweet, crunchy breakfast cereal. Other times she'll buy luscious desserts to take home for the family—and somehow they'll never make it home. One time she ate an entire cheesecake. Another time, she finished off two carrot cakes that she had bought for a party of her mother's.

Charisse does everything she can to control her secret eating. She buys desserts that she doesn't like—but she sometimes binges on them anyway. She makes sure her mother doesn't have much extra food in the house—but then she sneaks out late to an all-night grocery store. She's starting to feel like she has an entire secret life, one that fills her with shame and disgust.

Recently, Charisse heard about a girl who ate huge amounts of food and then made herself throw up right after, in order to keep from gaining weight. At first, the idea disgusted her even more, but lately she's beginning to think it might be a solution.

Similarities and Differences Among Compulsive Eaters

The first thing to notice about our three profiles is how different each girl is. Maggie and Luisa are heavy, while Charisse is of average weight. Maggie has close friends and a loving boyfriend, while Charisse keeps her distance from her friends and her dates and Luisa has no friends. Maggie eats openly, while Charisse eats secretly and Luisa eats both ways. Maggie and Luisa eat food they like, while Charisse binges on food that disgusts her. Luisa and Charisse get a great deal of attention from their families, while Maggie's family tends to leave her alone.

Clearly, each girl has her own set of feelings about food, weight, and eating, and her own reasons for her relationship to food. On the other hand, each girl definitely has something in common with the others: all three are using food to handle other emotional problems, and all three are frustrated because their solutions aren't working.

Like most compulsive eaters, Luisa is using food to work out many different feelings. First, she has been told that she's not allowed to express her anger. When her family teases her or makes demands on her, she's expected to go along cheerfully, without a thought for herself. So while she swallows her anger, Luisa also swallows food. It's as though she hoped that by stuffing food into herself, she could also stuff away the feelings that she is afraid to express.

Luisa is also not allowed to protect herself against the teasing she finds painful; she's been told not to get angry or tell the tease to stop. Instead of defying this family rule, Luisa accepts it—and protects herself by putting a wall of fat between herself and the rest of the world.

This helps explain why Luisa assumes that her fat is the reason that no one will be friends with her. As we saw with Maggie, it's perfectly possible for someone who is heavy to have good friends and an active dating life. But Luisa has learned from her family that when people get close to you, they hurt you with their teasing and their demands. Since she's agreed not to tell people to stop hurting her, the only protection she can imagine is to keep people at a distance.

Luisa has also gotten the message from her family that she's not supposed to have friends or activities outside the family. Luisa wants to be a good daughter, so she doesn't challenge this unspoken rule. At the same time, like most teenagers, she would like to have more independence from her family and more relationships that don't include them. And she doesn't want to face the fact that there's a conflict between what she wants and what her family wants.

So Luisa tries to pretend that there is no conflict—because she can't have friends outside the family anyway. She comes to believe that the reason for her isolation is not because she's going along with her parents' wishes, it's because she's too fat. Even though Luisa isn't consciously aware of it, she's using fat to prevent a conflict with her parents from ever having to emerge. And she's consoling herself for what she's giving up—friends and outside activities—by a secret life with food.

That's one of the reasons why diets and willpower don't work for compulsive eaters. If Luisa needs her fat to help prevent a conflict she's afraid of, she won't be able to force herself to lose weight. Her will to prevent the conflict through being fat is stronger than her will to lose weight.

Likewise, if Luisa is giving up her privacy and separateness from her parents in other areas, she needs her secret candy bar treats very much. They are the one place Luisa has said, "I have the right to privacy and I have the right to a life of my own." These are important, good impulses, even if they are getting expressed in unsatisfying ways.

If Luisa sees another solution to her dilemma, or if she becomes more willing to be in conflict with her parents, then she no longer has the same reason to eat secretly or to be fat. In that case, she may give up her secret eating, and she may lose some weight. Of course, since all of this is going on unconsciously, without Luisa realizing it, the first step is for her to become aware of her own feelings.

Maggie is using food and fat in quite a different way. Because Maggie desperately wants to be close to others, she doesn't use fat to keep them away. Thus, even though she has gained a great deal of weight, her friendships and dating life are not affected.

Of course, no matter what an individual's attitude might be, we are all affected by the dominant social attitude, which says that heavy or fat girls are not attractive. Some boys may not be willing to date girls that don't fit the prevailing thin image now in fashion. Yet it's also true that there are heavy girls who have no trouble finding good relationships with boys, so even if appearance is one factor in dating, it's clearly not the only factor.

Dating and close friendships aren't an issue for Maggie—but a sense of control over her own life is. She has said she wants to do something—eat less—but she can't do it. Unconsciously, Maggie is acting out something that she feels, but doesn't want to admit: that she feels very out of control of her relationships to her parents. Since their divorce, she isn't sure that she's welcome to live with either one of them. Since Maggie still loves and depends on her parents, this feeling is very frightening. It's so frightening that Maggie would rather not face it at all. But, as we've seen, feelings always come out somehow. Maggie's worries about being out of control aren't coming into her mind directly—but she's acting them out with her behavior toward food.

In Maggie's case, fat isn't a wall to keep people away—but it may be a way of feeling bigger and stronger. Because Maggie feels scared and helpless—after all, what will she do if her parents don't want her?—getting fat may seem like a way to become bigger and more powerful. Like Luisa, Maggie is using fat to pretend that there really is no conflict with her parents. So what if they don't want her—she's so big and strong, she doesn't need them anyway!

Again, dieting and willpower can't work for Maggie, because on this hidden level, she doesn't really want to lose weight. As long as she believes, unconsciously, that she needs the weight to keep her big and powerful, she will have a strong reason to stay fat. And as long as she's not allowing her fears of being out of control to come to the surface, she'll have a powerful reason to express them through eating.

What about Charisse, whose self-control is so strong that she has managed not to gain weight in spite of her frequent binges? Like Luisa, Charisse comes from a family that places very high expectations on her. In Luisa's case, the expectations take the form of putting the family's needs first. In Charisse's case, the expectations concern her performance and her appearance of being perfect.

Charisse has gotten a clear message from her family: if she can't appear perfect, they may not love her. Like most people, Charisse wants and needs her parents' love, so she's willing to go to great lengths to get it. But she's also frightened that she may not be able to be as perfect as her parents expect her to be. After all, she's only human!

In addition, Charisse is very angry about her parents' demands. She would like to think of her father as helpful and loving, but way down deep, his lack of faith in her really makes her mad. Why does he keep asking her to explain herself? Why can't he just accept her the way she is?

When Charisse gets mad, she immediately feels guilty. How can she feel this way about her father who loves her?

After all, he works hard to achieve his goals—why shouldn't he expect the same from her? Feeling guilty leads Charisse to expect to be punished. After all, she has done something bad—she has gotten mad at her father. In a sense, Charisse's eating binges are both a way of expressing her anger and a way of expressing her guilt. Instead of hurting her father, Charisse hurts herself, eating food she doesn't even like. Then she feels guilty about her loss of control and punishes herself by dieting even more rigidly than before.

Again, all of this is going on unconsciously. Charisse doesn't want to look at her feelings of anger and guilt; she would rather believe that her father is as perfect as he is supposed to be, and that she feels only love and respect for him. Charisse thinks that anger is an ugly feeling that should be kept secret. In a sense, she's acting out that feeling by eating in an "ugly" way and then keeping it secret.

Once again, Charisse can't solve her problem with mere willpower because lack of willpower is not the problem. The real problem is that in Charisse's mind, she is a bad person for having "bad" feelings about her father, so all of her willpower is summoned to cover up this unpleasant truth—through bingeing and dieting instead of screaming and shouting. In order to solve the real problem, Charisse will have to find a way that feels comfortable for her to express her feelings.

So as we end this chapter on compulsive eating, let's be very clear about what we're saying and what we're not saying. We're *not* saying that anyone who is heavy has emotional problems with food, although they very well may suffer from society's negative attitudes toward fat women. We are saying that all of us have to confront those attitudes, so we all have to find a way to challenge them, live with them, or negotiate with them. We all must find a relationship to weight that works for us, that allows us to accept ourselves and feel good about how we look, however we manage to do that. And we're saying that if a person *is* eating or dieting compulsively, whether or not this produces a weight gain, she would benefit from getting help in looking at the true source of the problem, so that she can go on to choose a more pleasant and satisfying relationship to food.

4

The Disease of Self-Starvation: Anorexia Nervosa

Which do you think is the healthier situation: to be 10%–15% above your ideal weight, or to be 10%–15% below it?

If you answered "below," you're not alone. Most people in this society believe that thinner is better—stronger, healthier, and more attractive. But in fact, many studies have shown that given the choice, it's better to be slightly over your ideal weight than slightly under it.

Even with that information, you might feel a conflict. A person might think, "Now I know it's healthier to weigh a little more but I still think I look better weighing a little less. And if I look better, I'll feel better—even if it isn't really as healthy!"

If you can understand that conflict, you can understand some of the way an anorexic feels. *Anorexics*—people who suffer from anorexia nervosa—never believe that they are thin enough. They may weigh only three-fourths of the weight that is normal for their height and build. They may faint regularly from lack of energy. To their family and friends, they look like prison-camp victims, so thin that you can see every rib.

To themselves, however, they are still "too fat." Even when anorexics are hospitalized for malnutrition, they will point to different places on their bodies, showing their doctors where they still need to lose weight.

In some ways, this tragic eating disorder is almost a logical extension of our society's preoccupation with women's thinness. Most women and girls worry about their weight. And most girls have unrealistic ideas about their bodies, believing they are fatter than they really are.

For example, in one study of 1,000 high school girls, about half said they were *obese*—seriously overweight. (The medical definition of *obese* is 25% above your normal weight as defined by a doctor.) In fact, according to accepted medical standards, only about one-fourth of those students were actually obese. The others had a distorted idea of their bodies.

Another study of healthy women, conducted by Suzanne Abraham and Derek Llewellyn-Jones and published in 1984, found that only 17% of them were happy with their present weight. Almost half (47%) wished they could be "a little lighter," and almost one-third (32%) wished they could be "a lot lighter." Only 1% wanted to be "a little heavier"!

This wish to be thin is especially difficult for teenage girls. Starting at about age 11, most teenage girls go through a growth spurt. This growth spurt requires a girl to eat more food than she ate before—and more food than she needs to eat after about age 14, when the growth spurt ends. If a girl does not change her eating habits when the growth spurt ends, she will probably gain some weight.

Of course, the teen years are also the time when a girl's body changes into a woman's. Most women develop breasts, hips, and other layers of fat. It's hard to make generalizations about men and women, but for the most part, women are biologically designed to have layers of fatty tissue that shape their bodies differently from men's.

Many hormonal changes take place during the teen years. These changes may affect a teenager's appetite, metabolism (how her body changes food into energy or into fat), and, at least temporarily, her weight. They may also affect her mood, how she feels about herself, and how she feels about her body.

For all these reasons, the teen years can be difficult ones. Your body, your eating habits, and your idea of yourself are all changing. Sometimes it can feel as if you're going through several changes in one day! These changes, combined with the overall message that women must be thin to be attractive, may make it hard for a teenager to feel comfortable with her body or her eating habits.

These are all pressures that most of us experience. Likewise, the teen years are a time when most of us are under many different kinds of pressures. Parents may expect us to act like adults while treating us like children. School standards get more difficult, along with new responsibilities of work, sports or other extracurricular activities. To some extent, all teenagers are looking for ways to cope with these pressures.

Where the anorexic is different, and why we call her pattern an eating *disorder*, is because she tries to deal with these pressures by starving herself. The anorexic goes beyond merely dieting in order to achieve and maintain a healthy weight. To the anorexic, no weight is ever low enough. No amount of food is small enough—she must constantly push herself to eat less and less.

Some anorexics—perhaps as many as 40%—have periods where they cannot maintain their rigid diets. They may *binge*—eat large amounts of food in a very short time. That's because, even while they are dieting, anorexics are preoccupied with food. After an anorexic goes on a binge, she may make herself throw up, to get rid of the food that she fears will make her fat. She may take a dangerous number of laxatives to purge herself. Or she may simply go back on her killing schedule of diet and exercise, trying desperately to make up for her "bad" eating. (Although this pattern may resemble bulimia, the anorexic is maintaining an abnormally low weight, while the bulimic's weight is within the average range.)

As we've seen, anorexics have something in common with other people who worry about their weight. But in a way, it's too simple to look at anorexics as ordinary dieters gone overboard. Most anorexics can be found in certain types of families, and they usually fit a certain personality type. This has led many researchers to conclude that anorexics are not only concerned with looks or weight. They are also severely troubled by other conflicts. Usually, they feel unable to control their lives as they would like. Therefore, they turn to the one area they believe they *can* control—their own bodies. Starving themselves to become thinner than anyone else may seem like the one "accomplishment" they can achieve.

Recognizing Anorexia

Sometimes it takes a long time for someone's family and friends to realize that a person has anorexia. That's partly because anorexics tend to hide the things they do to starve themselves. They may push food around on their plate during a family meal, pretending to eat. Or they may frequently have a "good reason" for missing family meals, claiming that they ate at another time. They may exercise late at night or hide themselves in the bathroom to throw up or to use laxatives.

Secretiveness and withdrawal from others are part of the pattern of anorexia. Because the anorexic is using her routines of diet, exercise, and purging to work through feelings that she is afraid to face, she tends to rely desperately on these routines. In fact, part of their purpose is to help her block out the world, a world that she finds too disturbing or frightening to face directly. This pattern of withdrawal may make it very difficult for others to realize how serious the situation is until it has gone quite far.

Many anorexics begin pulling away from those around them even before their eating disorder begins. In some cases, anorexics have been withdrawing from others for a year or more before they start to starve themselves. This period of withdrawal is actually a kind of warning sign of anorexia.

Sometimes anorexia develops slowly, but with so few warning signs that no one realizes what has happened until the anorexic has starved herself to the point where her condition is visible. Other times, an apparently sweet and friendly girl will suddenly become abrupt, even rude, in her rejection of friends and family. Whether gradually or suddenly, however, the anorexic has withdrawn from those around her.

Here are some other signs of anorexia. As we've discussed, some of them may seem common to many teenage girls, while others represent a medical extreme. If you or someone you know seems to have several of the characteristics on this list; if reading this list makes you uncomfortable and worried about yourself or somebody else; or if reading the list rings a bell with you in some way, pay attention. The person you're thinking of may well have anorexia—or be on her way to having it.

Possible Signs of Anorexia:[1]

- loss of 15% or more of normal body weight
- regularly taking in less than 1,000 calories a day
- *amenorrhea*—menstrual periods stop (a common sign of starvation, as the body cannot afford to lose nutrients through menstrual blood)

[1] Some signs of anorexia, including weight loss or loss of appetite, may be caused by serious illness, as well. We're assuming that these signs are being observed in an otherwise healthy person.

- refusal to maintain a minimum body weight
- seeing food as an enemy
- feeling that a diet has taken over one's life
- continual exercise, possibly late at night or at other odd times
- pacing around while eating
- rushing from the table to purge or vomit after eating or being forced to eat
- binges and/or binge-purge periods followed by periods of starvation
- continual fear of gaining weight
- considering oneself fat although others do not; being of apparently "normal" weight while obsessing continually about being fat
- intense fear of being overweight, even if one is not heavy or has been losing weight

Sometimes an anorexic begins her disorder by being of normal weight, gaining weight, and then trying in a panic to lose it. As she diets the initial weight gain away, she begins to become obsessed with diets, weight loss, and appearance. She doesn't stop her diet when she reaches her former normal weight but continues to diet and perhaps exercise obsessively. She may also use vomiting, laxatives, diet pills, and *diuretics* (medication that helps the body to lose water, usually through urinating) to help her lose weight.

Sometimes an anorexic is a former compulsive eater. She may indeed have been heavy, overweight, or even obese at one time. She may have lost a great deal of weight through dieting and continues to be obsessed with the fear that she will gain weight again, or even with the fear that she is still fat, no matter what the scale or her mirror tells her.

Of course, in our weight-obsessed society, these feelings are common among many women who are not necessarily anorexic. Although it might be helpful for these women to develop a more realistic image of their bodies or to examine their ideas about the importance of being thin, such women are still maintaining a normal body weight. These ideas are only part of anorexia; the other part is the actual deprivation of food to the point where the anorexic is endangering her health.

Whether or not the anorexic has ever been overweight, she's likely to find an exciting sense of power and control through dieting. Dieting, she discovers, means that she can decide how her body will look and what the scale will say. Although most people who intend to lose weight feel a sense of pleasure and power in achieving their goal, the anorexic is pleased out of all proportion to what has actually happened.

Most people recognize that losing weight will not guarantee success in school, work, or dating; it will not improve a troubled relationship or make family ties more pleasant or help one decide which career or college to choose. But the anorexic focuses on control over her weight as though it held the secret to all these other issues. In fact, the more she focuses on weight loss, the more she is able to push these other issues aside while triumphing in her sense of power over her body.

Sometimes weight loss and dieting help make the anorexic girl feel superior to other people. In this irrational reasoning, other people are weak and out of control because they have to eat, while the anorexic, who can eat little or nothing, has superior powers of control.

In this thinking, every day becomes a contest between the anorexic and her appetite, between the anorexic and all others who might eat less or weigh less than she does, and, most frequently, between the anorexic and people who are trying to make her eat. Ordinarily shy or accommodating girls may suddenly become fierce and stubborn: finally, they are refusing to do what others ask of them! If this is the one of the first times they have stood up for themselves, it may be an exhilarating feeling—even if it means they are risking death.

In fact, the anorexic whose condition becomes apparent to others may well receive a great deal of attention as worried friends and family try to coax her to eat in order to save her life. This attention may be quite welcome to the anorexic. Whether she's consciously aware of it or not, she may feel that she's finally gotten the control over other people that she never had before. Instead of being helpless and trying to please everyone else, she is now a powerful person whom others are trying to please. Furthermore, she's established herself—in her own mind—as a special person with a special goal that no one else could possibly understand. She may feel heroic, brave, and determined, as though she were capable of feats that others can only envy.

Of course, in order to gain this superior status, the anorexic has to deprive herself of many ordinary experiences. Eventually, the anorexic will avoid dating, times out with friends, family gatherings, schoolwork, sports, and all other activities—partly because she's too preoccupied with food and diet, partly because she's too physically depleted to think clearly or to lead a normal social life.

Some anorexics are only interested in food and dieting. This type of anorexic has a great deal of contact with others—but her conversations revolve exclusively around food, weight, and appearance. These anorexics may shop obsessively for special gourmet foods or demand that others buy such foods for them. They then refuse to eat the food, but continue to ask for such special treats.

Likewise, some anorexics seem obsessed with food and cooking. They collect recipes and prepare for their friends and family new treats that they themselves refuse to eat. An anorexic might spend hours in the kitchen preparing elaborate gourmet meals for her family—and then become furious when others would not eat *for* her. Other anorexics hoard the food that they refuse to eat, as though it were somehow precious and important—or perhaps as though it were ugly and distasteful, something that needs to be kept out of sight.

Sometimes the anorexic's obsession with food comes out in strange rituals of eating. The anorexic might cut her food into tiny pieces, count the number of times she chews or the number of bites she takes, drink a glass of water between every swallow of food, eat without a fork, or create some other special way of eating.

These rituals serve several purposes. First, they may help the anorexic to hide her self-starvation from those with whom she eats. The anorexic who is busily cutting up her food and who seems to be actively eating and drinking appears to be eating much more than she actually is.

Likewise, such rituals may help the anorexic to control her own hunger. Drinking water or diet soda may help her to feel full, even though she hasn't gotten the nutrition she needs. Taking excessive amounts of time over a meal may make it easier for the anorexic to eat less.

Beyond these "practical" reasons, however, rituals may help the anorexic believe that she has gained some new kind of control over her food—and therefore, over her life. She may come to believe that if she eats without a fork, the food doesn't count, or that if she follows the pattern she has set for herself, she has achieved an important victory.

Likewise, focusing energy and attention on the ritual means that the anorexic can ignore any other disturbing or painful feelings that she might have. Conflicts with her family or feelings that she believes won't be acceptable can remain hidden. Instead, she concentrates on cutting up a sliver of apple into 40 or 50 little pieces.

Some anorexics' rituals revolve around exercise as well as or instead of food. In these cases, the anorexic girl is afraid ever to stop exercising, for fear that the little food she has eaten will turn to fat. She may actually stay up all night, dancing or exercising. She may find a way to "exercise" even while sitting still, flexing her fingers or curling her toes while she sits at her desk. Or she may pace quickly around the room while eating, trying to counteract the effect of the food.

In such cases, it's almost as though the anorexic were afraid to be at rest. Again, such a girl may feel frightened of thoughts and feelings that seem unacceptable to her. Without consciously realizing it, she may feel that she has to be in constant motion to keep out these disturbing ideas.

As you remember, in Chapter 3 we talked about how compulsive eaters had lost touch with their own sense of hunger. Either they were eating foods that artificially distorted the hunger-full cycle—sweet, starchy foods—or they binged well past the point where they felt full, driven by other needs than hunger to keep on eating.

Likewise, anorexics have a distorted relationship to hunger. Whereas most people find hunger an unpleasant sensation and want to eat to relieve it, many anorexics are relieved by feeling hungry. To them, this feeling is a reassurance that they are not in fact gaining weight. Just as the compulsive eater may continue to stuff herself long after she feels full, the anorexic may feel bloated and "ready to explode" after even a modest meal. She comes to feel that her only safety is in a completely empty stomach.

Sometimes anorexics have distorted or irrational ideas about food and their bodies. One anorexic, for example, told her doctor that she was afraid that if she ate, the food would "never come out." Of course, this is biologically impossible—but it expresses the intense fear that the girl had attached to food.

As we've seen, the anorexic develops her obsession with food until her entire life revolves around what the scale says. An anorexic might maintain that she doesn't want to go to a party or out to a movie with a new friend. If she's asked "How can you be so sure you'll have a bad time?" she may well answer, "Because I feel fat." In other words, her entire experience is dependent upon her weight and her appearance.

Medical Effects of Anorexia

Ironically, although anorexia is a dangerous disorder that can lead to severe medical problems and even death, most anorexics deny these problems. They may be dizzy, exhausted, or regularly fainting from lack of nutrition, but they will continue to insist that they are not hungry, that they feel fine, that their only problems come from being "too fat."

The medical symptoms of anorexia are identical to the symptoms of starvation. That's because anorexics are, quite literally, starving themselves to death. The body can't tell whether starvation is voluntary or comes from an unavoidable shortage of food. It reacts in exactly the same way, no matter what the reason for its deprivation.

Physical Symptoms of Anorexia:
- dizziness
- loss of concentration
- irritability
- serious insomnia (inability to sleep)
- numbness in hands and feet
- depression—a feeling of hopelessness and despair, which the anorexic may attribute to her inability to lose weight, but which has other psychological roots as well as being a result of malnutrition
- infections that don't heal
- bruises—both because the body's resistance to any trauma is lowered and because when bones are unpadded by fat, the body bruises more easily
- low tolerance for cold weather—again because the body is missing its protective padding of fat
- a layer of fine, downy hair covering the body—seems to be the body's effort to protect itself from the cold when natural padding is lost
- low blood pressure
- irregular heartbeat
- heart failure
- dehydration (often exaggerated by the diuretics that many anorexics take to help them lose so-called water weight)
- kidney failure (dehydration puts a terrible strain on the kidneys, in addition to starvation-induced potassium shortages and other nutritional imbalances)

- lowered body temperature
- sunken eyes
- gray or yellowed skin, which is sometimes broken out
- dry, patchy hair (from a loss of protein)

Despite the physically unattractive qualities with which we've ended our list, many anorexics believe that they are more beautiful than they've ever been—because they have finally become almost as thin as they would like. Some flaunt their new, thin bodies, which to them are evidence of their stunning self-control and perhaps also of their superiority to others.

Other anorexics try to hide their thinness, fearing that if people find out what they've accomplished, they'll try to "spoil" it by forcing the anorexic to eat. To them, their superiority must stay a closely guarded secret, to defend them against the envy and ill wishes of others.

Whether an anorexic is proud or secretive about her new weight loss, she deeply distrusts anyone who wants to get her to eat. To her mind, the person who wants to feed her is actually trying to control her, to take her prized thinness and self-control away from her, to make her helpless and powerless once again. If her health becomes so poor that she is hospitalized, the anorexic regards the hospital as the ultimate betrayal.

Anorexics often focus on one part of their bodies, such as their hips, their stomachs, or their thighs. Even if they are down to 75 pounds and having to be hospitalized, they may still insist that this one body part is still fat, is still not yet perfect.

Some people think that anorexics genuinely believe that they are fat, even when they have become emaciated. Some recovered anorexics, however, in recalling their experience with the disorder, have said that they understood quite well that they weren't fat. They were simply afraid that if they admitted that, they would be forced to eat. Whatever their image of their bodies, it was important to them to continue their regimen of iron self-control and to maintain their low weights.

The long-term medical consequences of anorexia are quite severe. If an anorexic receives medical help in her disorder's early stages, she has a better chance of both ending the disorder and avoiding long-term medical problems as a result of it. Starvation, whatever its source, affects the brain, and it may have a particularly severe effect on adolescents, whose brain is still growing.

Anorexia has other long-term effects, as well. If an anorexic has been purging with laxatives for a month or more, her intestines may become unable to function on their own. If she stops taking laxatives, the waste may become impacted in her intestines and may have to be surgically removed.

Of course, the most severe long-term consequence of anorexia is death. Tragically, 2% to 21% of those who develop anorexia actually die of their self-starvation. Even if they are hospitalized, they may tear out the tubes that are feeding them internally or try to continue exercising in their emaciated condition. As we saw, they may view the hospital as a betrayal, a giant conspiracy designed to make them fat.

Although some people believe that the girls who become anorexics really want to die, in fact these girls have become convinced that they have no other option for survival. To such a girl's distorted way of thinking, certain feelings and ideas—such as anger, or criticism of her family—seem far more dangerous than the actual dangers she is inflicting on her body. If the anorexic can realize that her effort to control herself through starvation is actually going to destroy her, she may become motivated to accept help and begin treatment.

Who Is Anorexic?

Some 95% of all anorexics are women. The vast majority of them are from 12 to 18 years old, although this disorder has occurred in people as old as 40 or 50.

Anorexia is becoming an increasingly widespread condition. A few decades ago, it was virtually a textbook problem that emerged very rarely in real life. Over the past 20 years, however, this disorder has become a growing threat to high school and college students. Some researchers estimate that as many as one woman in 250 in the United States has anorexia. Other researchers place the figure as high as one in every hundred female students between the ages of 16 and 18.

This disorder can in some cases be maintained as a way of life for several years. In other cases, it leads to acute illness, which is either cured or which ends in death, as happens in an estimated 2% to 21% of all cases. Some estimates put the number of deaths as high as 3,750 per year.

Anorexia and Families

From what kind of families do anorexics come? Ironically, they're the families that on the surface seem to be the perfect, storybook families that other people envy. They tend to be upper-middle-class, with two biological parents (i.e., not families with a history of divorce or remarriage) and one or more healthy, attractive children.

Usually, anorexics come from small families, often with older parents who gave birth in their thirties or forties. There are usually not very many boys in an anorexic family, or the boys are very much younger than the girls.

The fathers in families of anorexics may have desperately wanted sons and are consciously or unconsciously disappointed in having had daughters instead. They may have developed unrealistic expectations for their daughters to make up for their disappointment.

Mothers in families of anorexics tend to be wrapped up in their own role as mothers of "ideal children." They are often very involved in every area of their daughters' lives, seeing themselves as giving and loving and expecting love and obedience from their daughters in return. Some mothers of anorexics gave up their own careers to devote themselves full-time to caring for their children, and they have turned their involvement with their daughters into a career of its own. Other mothers are themselves obsessed with weight and appearance, believing that "perfect" looks are extremely important.

The girls who develop anorexia are usually bright and pretty, as far as one can imagine from the typical "problem child." As we shall see, their development of an eating disorder may be the only way they know to express that something is wrong in their supposedly perfect families.

Anorexia rarely appears in poor or developing countries or in lower-income families in the United States. In areas where there might be genuine scarcity, either a lack of money or an actual lack of food, young girls don't seem to turn to self-starvation. This eating disorder seems to occur only in homes where there is enough to eat.

In fact, the conflict between appearance and reality may be part of the source of the anorexic's problem. While on a material level, there is enough, emotionally, the anorexic may be feeling starved or deprived. Her parents may insist that they love and cherish her, yet she may sense that they are really quite self-involved, that they value her more for her good grades and high performance than for herself, or that she is loved only when she is sweet and well-behaved but not when she is angry, frustrated, or unhappy.

The anorexic usually comes from a family where she is a model child. She is taught to set high standards for herself, to do well in many areas while being sweet and likeable. Like many girls, she is given the contradictory message that she should do well without seeming to try too hard: she should be tops in school, sports, or social activities but not seem competitive, aggressive, or self-satisfied.

The anorexic's family tends to expect their "model" daughter to prove herself continually. Although the family may see itself as loving and nurturing, it actually is quite demanding. The family may have unrealistically high expectations: everyone should get all A's, no one should ever be angry, other families have problems but we don't. Of course, no family is without problems. But if a family believes that it *should* be without problems, every member of that family is under a tremendous strain.

Anorexics' families may have an exaggerated fear of failure. Nobody likes to fail, but parents whose daughters become anorexic may be terrified of failure beyond all rational judgment. Just as the anorexic comes to believe that eating one piece of bread makes her bloated or "a fat pig," her parents may somehow believe that if they miss one promotion, give one unsuccessful party, or don't make friends with one particular person, they're complete failures.

In such an atmosphere, people are constantly comparing themselves to others. The children in such families are likewise under enormous pressure to be perfect, and they sense their parents' anxiety about failure—even if it is not spoken.

Of course, if your only standards come from making comparisons, you will find yourself coming out "behind" more often than not. Even if you are getting the best grades, dating the most popular guy, wearing the most stylish clothes, you will always be worried that tomorrow, someone else will come out "better." In this context, it makes sense that some girls might chose anorexia—a contest of no-eating in which they are sure to come out "ahead."

Girls who become anorexic are usually quite demanding of themselves, and consequently, quite self-critical. To such a girl, nothing she does is ever quite good enough. She may feel that days of being "nice" are wiped out by one unguarded moment when she loses her temper. Suddenly, her loving parents are angry with her, too, or turn cold and disappointed.

Or she may feel that her own needs are really not as important as her parents' needs or the needs of others in her family. Perhaps at the start of every school year, her parents sit down with her to help her plan her courses. They may all see this as loving, helpful counsel—but in reality, the girl may feel that her own interests are not as important as those of her parents; that to be a "good" girl, she should choose her schedule based on their advice rather than on her own wishes.

In such a context, the girl who becomes anorexic may be afraid to choose an active, open way of rebelling. She may feel too guilty or frightened to say, "I'm not going to do what you want—I'm going to do what I want." She may not even like to imagine that she could have thoughts or feelings that would contradict her parents or their image of the supposedly happy family they all share.

But feelings will always come out in one way or another. If a girl will not directly express her feelings of anger, rebelliousness, and wanting to do things her own way, she will find a way to express them indirectly, maybe without even realizing it. The anorexic chooses to express these upsetting feelings through her efforts to diet and to control her body. In effect, without having to say so directly, she is communicating a powerful message: I am a separate person from you, and I can do what I like with my own body.

The typical image that the anorexic tries to present—whether consciously or unconsciously—is that of the perfect, fragile little girl. As we've seen, girls don't develop anorexia until they are about to become teenagers—until they are on their way to becoming women. The little girl who was happy to involve her mother in all of her choices struggles with new decisions as she becomes a teenager. The child who found it easy to get good grades becomes the teenager who must not only get good grades but develop an impeccable school record that will get her into a top college. The little girl who found it easy to be "daddy's pet" becomes a teenager with conflicting feelings that include "unacceptable" anger and frustration.

The change from childhood to adolescence creates new conflicts and problems in all families. But it creates special strains in the families of girls who become anorexic because the parents in these families may be intolerant of independence, anger, and "failure" in their children. Part of becoming a teenager is searching for independence, trying out new things—sometimes failing, sometimes succeeding. Part of being a teenager is also having a wide variety of feelings, including anger, resentment, sadness, and other feelings that don't go with the image of being perfect. If these parts of being a teenager are not acceptable in a family, the teenager may respond by becoming anorexic.

Profiles of Anorexics

Here are three composite profiles of anorexic girls. These are not the stories of actual girls, but the combination of many actual stories into three portraits that represent the important aspects of anorexic girls and their families.

Kira, age 15, has always worked hard at her schoolwork and at her ballet dancing. She dreams of being a professional dancer and is willing to work hard for this goal.

Kira's parents are proud of their daughter. Kira's mother always wanted to be a dancer herself, but gave up dancing when she married Kira's father at age 17. Although she says she loves Kira's father, she has also told Kira that Kira should wait to get married until she has established herself in ballet. She and her daughter spend time together shopping for Kira's ballet clothes and shoes, looking at dance magazines, and imagining what it will be like when Kira is a famous ballerina.

"I missed my chance, but I'll have it again through you," Kira's mother often says. Once Kira asked her mother what would happen if Kira couldn't become famous. "Don't even let those negative thoughts into your head—that's the way bad things happen!" Kira's mother answered. Kira got the message that not being a dancer was the worst thing that could possibly happen—to her and to her mother.

Kira loves dance and accepts that her dedication to ballet sometimes means missing out on some of the social activities that her friends enjoy. Even though she doesn't go to as many social events as her friends do, she is quite popular and stays in good touch with her friends. Although she doesn't have a steady boyfriend, she goes out on dates when she has time.

Lately, Kira is beginning to worry whether she can achieve as much as she wants to in dance. She has been unusually clumsy in class lately. She is usually her teacher's favorite, but because she has made a few mistakes, she has the impression that her teacher is now giving more attention to a couple of the other students.

One day, Kira gets on the scale and notices that she has gained a pound and a half. She was both upset and relieved: this must have been the reason she had been having a hard time in dance class. She reasoned that as soon as she lost this unwanted weight, she would be back to her old place at the head of the class.

Meanwhile, Kira thought that she must hide her "ugly" body or her dance classmates will notice and tease her. In fact, in the competitive world of ballet, there is a lot of teasing and comparison of weight and bodies, so Kira's fears are to some extent realistic.

However, even when Kira lost the pound and a half, she couldn't stop being frightened. She worried about what might happen if she gained it back again. The only way to be sure, she reasoned, was to lose some more weight, so that she could always have a safety margin. Kira did lose more weight—but her performance in dance class did not improve. The only thing to do now, Kira reasons, is lose more weight.

Alexis, age 17, has always been her father's favorite. When she does well in school or in sports, she rushes home to tell her father, who praises her enthusiastically. When she does badly, her father is always there to comfort her. "You'll do better next time," he says. "In fact, I know *how* you'll do better—let's go out this Saturday and practice your backhand for a few hours," or "I'll come home from work early tomorrow and we'll spend the evening going over your algebra. You can get it if you work!" Alexis feels proud to have such a special dad.

Alexis is also proud of her mother, who looks much younger than her actual age of 45. Other girls had to fight with their mothers for permission to shave their legs or wear makeup—Alexis's mother actually came to her, offering to teach her how to do these "grownup" things. When Alexis gets ready to go out on a date, her mother comes in and checks her over. Sometimes she offers to lend Alexis another shade of eye shadow or a new lipstick that she thinks will go better with Alexis's clothes. Alexis's friends can't believe how lucky she is to have such an understanding, helpful, and attractive mother.

Alexis has always had a steady boyfriend and a couple of friends that she hangs out with. Her boyfriends have always been handsome and popular, like her.

Then Alexis has a run of bad luck. She sprains her ankle and has to drop out of a tennis tournament that she'd been practicing for for weeks. She and her boyfriend have a fight and Alexis hears from a girlfriend that he's been seen out with another girl. Alexis is in pain from her ankle and upset about her boyfriend, so she has a hard time studying for her college prep math course—and gets a B-minus on a pop quiz, an unusually low grade for her.

All of a sudden, it seems to Alexis that her life is ruined. Nothing is going right. She feels helpless, upset, and out of control.

Alexis has always observed a strict diet but suddenly, her diet is even stricter. First she cuts out her morning toast. Then she cuts out her morning juice so that all she is having for breakfast is a cup of coffee with milk. Then she starts drinking her coffee black.

Alexis notices that even with her stricter diet, she hasn't lost any weight. That's because, with a sprained ankle, she isn't getting the exercise that she's used to. But Alexis panics. She begins to worry that she has already gotten fat, even though she hasn't actually gained any weight—she just hasn't lost any. She imagines that her mother and father are secretly aware of her weight "problem" and just aren't saying anything about it because they feel too sorry for her. She's sure that if she can just manage to lose a little weight, things will be back to normal.

Alexis starts taking smaller portions for lunch and dinner. It becomes a game—how little can she take? She doesn't want her parents to see how hard she has to work to do such a simple thing as lose weight, so she tries to camouflage her reduced portions by talking a great deal at mealtimes, pushing her food around on her plate, cutting her food into smaller and smaller pieces, chewing each piece of food for 20 times, then 30 times, then 40 times.

Finally, the already thin Alexis loses five pounds—but she doesn't really feel any better. Her ankle is healed by now, but she has still missed the tennis tournament and now the season is over. Her boyfriend is still going out with other girls, and Alexis is sure all her friends are secretly laughing at her, even though they don't say anything about it to her face. She's still having trouble with math, partly because the work has gotten much harder, partly because hunger is making it difficult for her to concentrate.

Alexis decides that if she can just lose another five pounds, she'll have her life back in control. She starts skipping meals, hiding this fact from her parents with elaborate excuses that seem to work: she tells them she's studying and snacking in her room during mealtimes, that she'll eat later at a friend's house, or that she has an upset stomach today.

Alexis also steps up her exercise routine. She begins jogging five miles every morning. Then she adds another five miles in the evening before she goes to bed. She starts to think of ways that she can exercise while studying. Meanwhile, she wears loose clothing to hide her growing weight loss.

Leonie is 12 years old. She gets along all right with her parents, but sometimes they make her mad. Her father is always teasing her, calling her "Little Butterball," and slapping her on the bottom. If she says, "Daddy, I'm not fat," he says, "Don't worry, I like women with meat on them." If she gets mad, her mother takes her aside and gently explains that her father is only teasing and there's no reason to be upset.

Leonie's father's teasing makes her mad, but it also makes her very uncomfortable. Now that she is developing breasts, he teases her about those, too, saying things like "I guess June is busting out all over," or "Our little girl is going to break a lot of boys' hearts if she keeps on the way she's going." Leonie knows her breasts are bigger than a lot of other 12-year-old girls', but she doesn't know how to handle this kind of attention. Her mother never says anything to her father about it, but she very gently scolds Leonie if Leonie says anything.

A lot of Leonie's friends worry about weight and talk about new diets that they've read about in teen magazines. Leonie and a couple of her friends decide to go on a diet together. For one week, they will cut out all desserts.

Leonie's mother is an excellent cook and is quite proud of her cooking. At first, when Leonie says she wants to go on a diet, Leonie's parents think it's "cute." "Our little girl thinks she's ready to go on a diet!" says Leonie's father. "It's just a phase, it will pass," says Leonie's mother. She tries to make all of Leonie's favorite foods to tempt her not to keep this new resolution.

Leonie just smiles and sticks to her guns. For one whole week—no desserts! Even when her mother brings *three* of her favorite desserts to the table at once, Leonie manages just to sip a glass of milk. At the end of the week, Leonie feels triumphant, as though she has won an important contest.

So the next week, Leonie continues her diet and subtracts other things—bread, potatoes, and pasta. Her mother is even more puzzled and upset. Her father takes Leonie aside and asks her why she's upsetting her mother. Leonie just smiles. "I love Mom—I just want to lose some weight," she says. "All the girls I know are on this diet."

The next week, Leonie cuts her portions in half. No matter how much food her mother piles on her plate, Leonie will only eat part of it. Leonie's parents are really worried now, but Leonie says the new diet is making her feel better.

Although each story is different, all three girls have one thing in common: each is trying to gain more control over her life through dieting and losing weight. Kira and Leonie are well on their way to becoming anorexic, while Alexis has already developed a fairly severe eating disorder. If these girls and their families don't receive treatment, the girls could continue to progressively starve themselves, with dangerous results.

Kira is in a field—dance—in which many people develop eating disorders. That's because weight actually is a key factor in this field, beyond the ordinary focus that it takes on in people's social lives. It's true that heavy ballerinas are not acceptable and that how a ballerina looks is considered to be closely related to how she dances.

Kira's sudden difficulty with dance may have several explanations. Sometimes, teenagers go through growth spurts that upsets their balance or their ability to move gracefully. Sometimes, indeed, promising young dancers turn out to be unable to fulfill their promise. It's unclear how serious Kira's problem is, whether she's just experiencing a temporary setback or actually realizing the death of her dream.

In either case, however, Kira's problem is not caused by weight, and it won't be cured by dieting. But Kira has learned that any defeat or difficulty is a terrible failure and cannot be allowed. She has also learned that her mother will be terribly disappointed if she, Kira, "fails." Kira's problem may be beyond her control—but Kira is terrified of accepting that reality. She would rather try to regain control through focusing on dieting.

Alexis's family has also taught her that failure, disappointment, and defeat are unacceptable. When Alexis has any sort of trouble at all, her father's immediate response is to try to help. While this seems to be a loving and helpful gesture, it actually gives Alexis the message that setbacks are frightening and must be avoided at all costs. Alexis's coming in second is such a terrible event that her father is willing to spend hours of time to prevent it ever happening again.

Likewise, Alexis's mother's apparently loving concern with Alexis's appearance has given Alexis an exaggerated idea of how important looks can be. By carefully evaluating Alexis's appearance before every date, Alexis's mother is giving the message that looks are so important, they require constant care and attention. Alexis's mother is so concerned with looking attractive herself, that Alexis can't imagine how terrible it must be to "fail" at looking good.

Leonie's problem is slightly different. She feels uncomfortable with her father's teasing, but is not allowed to protect herself from it. Although Leonie senses that there is something sexual and inappropriate in her father talking about her breasts, her mother is not supporting her in this perception. So Leonie has to find her own way of avoiding the thing that makes her uncomfortable. Her solution is to starve herself until the breasts go away.

Through her diet, Leonie has also found a way of saying "no" to her parents. Leonie's deciding to go on a diet with her girlfriends wasn't necessarily a danger. Many teenage girls go on diets together. But Leonie's mother's reaction shows how much she wants to have control over Leonie's every move. She can't tolerate the idea that her daughter made a decision with her friends instead of with her parents. Leonie realizes that here is one area where she can say to her parents, "I'll do what I want, not what you want."

The sad thing for all three girls is that the ways they've chosen to express their anger, disappointment, frustration, and wish for independence will only create more problems. If Kira continues to starve herself, her dancing will get worse, not better. Alexis's anorexia has already meant avoiding other chances to find another boyfriend and has interfered with her ability to concentrate on her studies. Leonie may win the battle over food with her parents but her victory could put her in the hospital.

On the other hand, with treatment, these girls and their families can find other ways of working out these conflicts, ways that get at the real problems and don't rely on food or dieting as a coverup. They can go on to resolve their problems in ways that may still involve pain and disappointment, but which also bring new possibilities for power and effectiveness in their lives.

5

The Binge-Purge Cycle: Bulimia

As we've seen, for most women, the "perfect" body is out of reach. That's because, at this time in our culture, the female body image most admired is that of the slender pre-teenager, before she has developed hips or full breasts.

In the past few years, a more buxom female image has started to come back into fashion. Even that image, however, goes along with the slender legs and a flat stomach, a look that may be physically difficult for big-busted girls to attain.

The Hollywood stars and fashion models who represent this perfect image spend a great deal of time working at it. They may actually have surgery to remove "extra" fat or even take out one or two ribs. Even without such extreme measures, they spend hours each day with personal trainers, working out, getting herbal wraps, and going through other types of effort to maintain their "perfect" bodies.

This hard work doesn't show in their image, of course. Their looks are supposed to appear effortless. We aren't supposed to notice the time, money, and work that went into achieving them. And so when we compare ourselves to them, we wonder what's wrong with us.

As we've seen, this pressure to have an unrealistically thin body can contribute to the development of eating disorders. Ironically, some of these stars themselves suffer from eating disorders. The singer Karen Carpenter became so obsessed with her weight that she developed anorexia, which led to her death. For many years, the actress Jane Fonda had a history of bulimia, bingeing and then purging to maintain her movie-star looks. It's interesting to notice that the pressures of having a "perfect" body spare no one—not even the models and movie stars who seem to set the standards.

Bulimia and the Perfect Facade

Although all the eating disorders we've examined suggest a concern with body image and appearance, in some ways, the bulimic is most concerned with these things. At least, she's most concerned with presenting herself as successful. If the anorexic gives the impression of being a perfect, fragile little girl, the bulimic tries to appear as the perfect, elusive, successful woman.

Bulimia gets its name from two Greek works: *bous*, which means "cow" or "ox" and *limos*, which means "hunger" or "famine." As the name signifies, bulimia is a disorder in which people feel a terrible hunger, as though they had been starving in a famine. They try to satisfy this hunger by eating "like a cow"—huge quantities of food, up to ten times the usual amount at one time.

Then, in dire fear of gaining weight, the bulimic makes herself throw up. Although she has given in temporarily to what she sees as her "disgusting, animal" side, throwing up allows her to regain control and to maintain her slender, attractive image.

Ironically, the bulimic is usually quite successful in her work, school, and social life. Neither her behavior nor her appearance gives any sign of her eating disorder.

As we've seen, eating disorders tend to be related to one another. Compulsive eating may become compulsive dieting, which may in turn may become anorexia, or self-starvation. Likewise, either compulsive eating or anorexia may become bulimia. In fact, as many as half of all known anorexics later become bulimic. That's because people with eating disorders have one thing in common: they are all engaged in a constant battle around food.

A bulimic may have relaxed eating habits when she is not bingeing, or she may try to live on a rigidly controlled diet. She may feel that any break in her diet will lead to a binge, or her binges may be triggered by non-food-related events, such as anxiety over an exam. Most bulimics are of average weight, give or take 10 or 15 pounds. Whatever their actual weight, however, they tend to share an intense fear of becoming fat.

As the pressure to be thin has increased, the incidence of bulimia is increasing. Although anorexia has received more publicity because of its dramatic, horrifying results, bulimia is actually more widespread.

Ironically, this disorder is also spreading as it receives more publicity. When some girls hear about the binge-purge cycle, they react not to the dangerous, even life-threatening aspects of the disorder, but to the prospect of eating as much as they want without gaining weight.

Of course, most people binge from time to time. Most people have had the experience of, say, eating a pint or two of ice cream at one sitting, or having seconds and thirds of a favorite meal until they were so stuffed they couldn't move.

The bulimic binges like this at least once a week and may even binge more often. A binge ranges from 1,000 to 20,000 calories at a time.

Binges may last for hours, or for days. They may involve favorite foods from childhood, foods that the bulimic is trying to avoid on her regular diet, or repellent foods that the bulimic normally doesn't crave. In any case, the foods are usually sweet and/or starchy.

A bulimic may eat three meals in a row, one right after another, or go from store to store buying treats and bingeing on them. She may try all sorts of tricks to keep herself from bingeing, such as hiding food from herself, locking it up, keeping no food in the house, pouring kitchen cleanser on food, or burying food at the bottom of the trash. When the bulimic is compelled to binge, however, she will always find a way to get more food, or to find, clean, or dig up the food she has hidden or tried to spoil.

Because she vomits after eating, the bulimic may be physically able to eat even more food than the compulsive eater. She may even have to steal money to support her habit. In extreme cases, some women have turned to prostitution to pay for their binges.

Like most other people with eating disorders, bulimics tend to have good days and bad days. A good day is when the tendency to binge has been controlled. A bad day is when the bingeing seemed to take over. Some bulimics go for days without bingeing and then give in. Others report the almost constant frustration of making it through each day without bingeing—only to give in every night and binge around supper time or after they've gone to bed.

In general, anorexics tend to develop their disorder in their early teens. Bulimics tend to be somewhat older, in their late teens or early twenties (although some women have or develop bulimia as late as in their fifties). In general bulimics tend to be successful—good students, popular kids, apparently well-adjusted at home. Frequently, bulimics also struggle with addictions to alcohol or drugs, as well as with their apparent addiction to their eating disorder.

Recognizing Bulimia

Following are some possible signs of bulimia. Unlike anorexia or compulsive eating, bulimia usually has little relation to weight, so it may be a more difficult disorder to detect. Its difficulty is compounded by the fact that most bulimics are extremely secretive about both their binges and their purges. Nevertheless, these warning signs may provide some clues.

Possible Signs of Bulimia:
- binges followed by severe diets, vomiting, laxatives, enemas, diuretics (medication to lose water weight), or extreme exercise
- constant fear of being fat, although weight is within 15 pounds of average
- fear of not being able to stop eating
- fear of eating without purging
- fear of losing control around food
- depression
- putting oneself down after a binge
- irregular menstrual periods
- tooth decay (from the acid in the vomit)
- unusual weight changes
- swollen salivary glands (giving the face a puffy, "chipmunk-like" look), dizziness, cramps

How Bulimia Progresses

Most bulimics begin their disorder with a tendency to binge. Frequently, they feel intense anxiety that is temporarily calmed by eating. Because bulimics are concerned with keeping their weight down, however, they are unwilling to give in freely to their impulses to eat.

A bulimic may binge uncontrollably and then try to regain control by dieting rigidly for a while. Or she may be able to control her bingeing as long as she knows that it will lead to gaining weight.

In either case, once the bulimic discovers the idea of purging, this appears as a solution. Perhaps the bulimic vomited accidentally and then realized that self-induced vomiting could help her avoid gaining weight. Perhaps she read about other bulimics or figured out the idea for herself. No matter how it began, knowing that she can prevent weight gain makes it even more difficult for the bulimic to resist her tendency to binge.

Bulimics describe their binge-purge cycle as a constant battle for control. Bingeing is when you are out of control; purging is when you regain that control. Some bulimics begin by bingeing only occasionally, then progressing up to several binge-purge cycles a day. Others continue to binge and purge a few times a month or a few times a week, but they live in the constant fear of the next loss of control.

Bulimia may progress rapidly to where it is an active medical threat, or it may become a way of life for several years, with severe long-term consequences. In general, the sooner the disorder is treated, the more successful and lasting treatment is likely to be.

Some bulimics begin their purges with laxatives, which seem like a less violent means of getting rid of food than vomiting. However, laxatives don't really prevent weight gain. By the time a laxative works, the food has already been digested and absorbed into the system. Voiding the bowels in this case may lead to a slight loss in water weight, but the food has had its effect.

Bulimics may be aware of this, and yet still behave as though the laxatives were helping them to lose weight. They may become dependent on laxatives for normal bodily functions. They may even begin to abuse laxatives, using as many as 20 to 200 per day. They may also abuse diuretics, enemas, and other procedures, even though these too do not really affect weight—all for the feeling of being in control.

If a bulimic is insistent on both bingeing and maintaining a low weight, she will eventually have to find a way other than use of laxatives and diuretics to lose weight. Most bulimics, as we've seen, turn to vomiting, whether or not they use other means. The 5% of bulimics that are male tend to avoid vomiting, but turn instead to vigorous exercise to cover up the effects of their binges.

Possibly there are more male bulimics than we know of because a man who exercises compulsively may not realize that he has an eating disorder, whereas a woman who vomits regularly cannot avoid knowing that something is wrong. However, female bulimics tend to see their problems as evidence of personal failure, rather than understanding that bulimia is a common eating disorder for which treatment is available. Rather than seeking help, the bulimic may simply feel increased contempt for herself.

Some bulimics turn to diet pills to control their appetites. But, because their binges are not triggered by hunger, appetite suppressants are usually unsuccessful.

Bulimics have described their binges as an escape from all feeling. Afterward, they may feel intense shame at their loss of control. They may be disgusted with themselves, feel guilty, hate themselves, or fear that their behavior will be discovered. While they are bingeing, however, their only focus is on food and eating. Temporarily, they feel calm and experience some sense of relief from the anxieties that triggered the binge.

Because food seems to be the only thing that works to calm her anxieties, the bulimic's entire day may become structured around food. She may need to know that before or after a difficult experience, she'll be able to binge, then purge, to calm herself down. Or she may fear the many opportunities to binge throughout the day, figuring out elaborate strategies for avoiding food. Some bulimics are terrified of eating anything without purging afterward and so must always ensure that they have a secret place to purge.

Some bulimics binge on impulse or in response to a specific event, such as a test or a big date. Still others have routines or rituals for their binges, although they may believe that their eating is accidental. They may just "happen" to pass a bakery or a delicatessen on the way home, and just "happen" to stop in and buy huge quantities of food. Even though they haven't admitted these routines to themselves, they may become intensely anxious at the thought of missing their favorite foods.

Many bulimics have a long history of battling their weight, with a long string of diets, diet pills, exercise regimes, and other weight-control attempts behind them. They may have once been heavy and live in fear of ever being fat again. Or they may see their life as a perpetual battle to keep weight off or to keep a five-pound weight gain from turning into real obesity. Many bulimics suffer from the so-called yo-yo syndrome of constantly gaining and then losing 5, 10, or 15 pounds. They may see life as a struggle between the pleasures of eating as they like and the need to control their appetites in order to control their weight. In such a context, bingeing and then purging can seem like the solution to a dilemma.

On the other hand, some bulimics come from a background of anorexia. Although they realize that they need to begin eating again, they still have an intense fear of becoming fat. Although they achieve the normal weight that anorexics fall below, they rely on purges to make sure that their normal weight doesn't turn into overweight.

"Bulimarexics" may have had a history of bingeing even as anorexics; the only difference is that now, they are repeating the binge-purge cycle at a manageable weight instead of at starvation level. In fact, Abraham and Llewellyn-Jones estimate that 40% of all anorexics binge while starving themselves. This group is most likely to become bulimic. Interestingly, the same researchers have found that only 10% of people who are obese binge. Contrary to the stereotype of the troubled fat person and the healthy thin one, it may be that people of normal and low weights are more likely to have troubled relationships to food.

Medical Effects of Bulimia

The medical consequences of bingeing and purging are quite severe. The bulimic's image of vomiting is that it erases the eating that preceded it, leaving no trace. In fact, repeated vomiting puts a considerable strain on the human system, and bulimics suffer many negative consequences from their purges.

When bulimics fast as well as purge, they are putting an additional strain on their livers. Fasting appears to the body as an emergency, as though no food were available and starvation were a possibility. As we saw in Chapter 2, the body tries desperately to maintain a stable level of blood sugar. With no new food coming into the system to provide blood sugar, the body turns to its own liver, where glucose—a kind of sugar—is stored.

However, after only a day of fasting, this store is used up. The dieter's image of fasting is that the fat somehow melts away. In fact, the body finds nutrients not in fat but in its own organs and muscle tissue. These are depleted first. Only if the fast continues for several days will the body turn to its deposits of fat—and then to muscle.

Fasting is particularly dangerous for teenagers, because their bodies are still growing. They need food, not only to maintain their daily levels of blood sugar but to allow their bodies to grow and develop. A bulimic teenager who fasts as well as purges is putting her system under a strain as well as preventing her own growth.

Some Medical Consequences of Bulimia:
- fatigue
- sore throat
- ulcerated esophagus (that is, sores on the tube that leads from the mouth to the stomach, through which the vomit passes; in severe cases, the esophagus lining may rupture, causing death)
- tooth decay (teeth rotted from the acid in the vomit)
- heart disturbances (from nutritional imbalances)
- infected salivary glands (leading to a swollen face)
- dry skin from loss of fluids (especially if the bulimic takes diuretics or laxatives)
- rash or skin eruptions
- dehydration (loss of bodily fluids)
- constipation (related to insufficient fluid)
- edema, or water retention (the body's response to being deprived of fluids—trying to hold onto them)
- electrolyte imbalances (incorrect amounts of sodium and potassium in the system, which can lead to muscle spasms, kidney problems, or heart failure)
- abdominal cramps

In addition, some bulimics abuse a very dangerous drug, Ipecac, which is normally used to induce vomiting in toddlers who have swallowed poisonous chemicals. Ipecac remains in the body's cells forever and can cause death if taken regularly for as short a time as a few weeks.

Who Develops Bulimia?

Unlike anorexia, which is found primarily in upper-middle-class homes, bulimia is found at all economic levels. And, as we've seen, this disorder is becoming more and more widespread. In the late 1970s, some 15% to 30% of the female college students surveyed in various studies were found to be bulimic. A later study, done by Dr. William Davis in 1981, found that 5% of all adult women in the U.S. suffer from bulimia.

As we've seen, most bulimics are attractive, successful women with no apparent weight problems. However, according to Abraham and Llewellyn-Jones, some 20% of bulimics abuse alcohol or drugs.

Bulimics usually first develop their disorders between the ages of 15 and 24, although it's possible to develop this disorder in one's thirties, forties, or fifties. Some 90% of all bulimics overeat in some way before they begin to binge, which helps account for their exaggerated concern with weight.

Frequently, a bulimic will develop her disorder at a transition point: when she goes away to school, starts a new job, ends or begins a significant relationship, or faces a change in her family circumstances. The additional anxiety of the change will provoke a round of bingeing, which in turn will lead the bulimic to find a way of "getting rid of the" effects of the binge.

Bulimics and Their Families

It isn't possible to lead a life that is completely free of anxiety. Every activity has some risks, and every commitment brings with it some stress. Most people feel anxious and tense some of the time. The teen years may be an especially anxious time as you try to sort out your growing choices and responsibilities.

Every life has some tension in it—but bulimics may have been given messages at home that make handling tension especially difficult for them. They may feel under pressure to live up to parents' high expectations, to remain always cheerful and enthusiastic, or even somehow to become perfect. If they have gotten the message that doubts, fears, and ordinary human failings are unacceptable, they must look for a way to hide these "shortcomings" while continuing to appear perfect.

It's painful enough to feel anxious, needy, or desperate. But if you are afraid to admit that you have these feelings and need to appear calm and perfectly in control at all times, the strain may seem unbearable.

In these circumstances, bingeing and purging may appear to be a solution. A bulimic may look down on herself for her eating pattern, but that contempt may seem preferable to admitting her real fears and frustrations.

Bulimics often come from families that put a great deal of stress on outward appearances. They are encouraged to look to others for approval, rather than using their own standards of judgment. Sometimes, however, others cannot be pleased. That reality is especially painful for the girl who becomes a bulimic. She may spend hours brooding over a teacher's critical remark or days worrying about an argument with a friend. Bingeing may come to seem like the only escape from these worries—and then purging seems like the only way to hide the binge.

Often the girl who becomes a bulimic reports that she didn't get sufficient care when she was a child. She may have lived with parents who seemed to fit the role of good parents, but who may have been too preoccupied with their own problems to really focus on those of their child. The girl who becomes bulimic may have been given the message that her parents were too busy, frightened, or insecure to help her with her problems, so that she had to learn early to rely on herself. At the same time, she was probably expected to continue the appearance of being part of a happy, loving family.

Most children go along with what their parents expect in some way or another. That's because a child is dependent on her parents and needs a parent's love and care to survive. So if a child is asked to pretend that she's getting taken care of properly, she will do so, even if deep down she feels deprived of attention or support. In fact, many children decide to blame themselves. They think that if they are feeling lonely, left out, or insecure, it's not because their parents are preoccupied elsewhere but because something is wrong with *them*. Thus, the girl who becomes bulimic may feel that something is wrong with her for living in such a happy, successful family and still feeling that something is missing.

Such a girl may learn to rely on herself, but perhaps only at the cost of denying her own needs. She may fear that if her parents find out how needy she is—or how angry she feels when they aren't available—they will stop loving her altogether. So she hides both her neediness and her anger, even from herself. Later, these hidden feelings may come back in the form of bingeing and purging.

Some researchers believe that the mothers of bulimic girls express concern over their own ability to be capable adults. Although they are parents, charged with the responsibility of bringing up a daughter, they themselves feel insecure and uncertain about their ability to live up to this job. This may lead to a great deal of anxiety of *their* part whenever their child makes a demand, as they worry about being able to give their child what she needs.

Ironically, the child may get the message that there is something ugly or bad about her needs because they seem to upset her mother so much. The mother's very worries have created just the problem that she worried about.

In other cases, the mothers of bulimics are distant and disapproving, or impossibly hard to please. The daughter gets the message that whatever she does, it will never be good enough to please her mother.

Sometimes this message is given in quite a subtle way. The mother frequently says how much she loves and admires her daughter, but nevertheless, the daughter senses that something is wrong. If she goes to hug her mother, for example, the mother may draw back, saying, "You know I just fixed my hair—don't mess it up," or "Not now, I'm washing the dishes." Even if the mother adds, "But thank you for the nice thought, darling," or "You certainly look lovely today," the daughter has gotten the message that there is something wrong with her need for love and affection. This message is all the more painful if no one in the family will acknowledge it, because the daughter is left doubting her own instincts while feeling more left out than ever.

Similar family studies suggest that the fathers of bulimics are frequently uninvolved in child-rearing. Instead, they are preoccupied with their own careers, which tend to be quite demanding. Such fathers demand a high level of performance from themselves—and also from their daughters. They often don't accept weakness in themselves, nor do they tolerate it in their children.

Generally, the parents of bulimics expect their daughters to be both beautiful and successful. They emphasize both appearance and performance, while also wanting their daughters to remain sweet and ladylike. The bulimic daughter tries to meet this impossibly contradictory set of expectations—and for a while, she may even succeed. The price she pays, though, is a pressing anxiety that comes out in the binges and purges that we have seen.

Profiles of Bulimics

Following are three composite studies of girls with bulimia. None of the three girls actually exist. But each girl's story includes several common features of bulimia.

Ana is 18 and a senior in high school. Although she always ends up succeeding at whatever she takes on, she always worries that she won't be able to. Her girlfriends are always laughing and shaking their heads because they can't understand how someone as smart and talented as Ana can worry so much about failing. They tease Ana about always asking for everybody's opinion about everything before she makes up her own mind.

Ana's parents own a bodega, a small grocery store, of which they're very proud. They're the first people in their family to own a business, and ever since Ana can remember, the entire family has worked long hours in the store.

Ana has always understood that the store came first, and that she should come to her parents for help only if it's very important. Her parents are very loving and affectionate when they do pay attention to her, but most of the time they seem preoccupied and worried about how the store is doing. Ana understands that it's hard work running a small business, and she does what she can to help out.

Although they are busy with the store, Ana's parents still have strong household rules for how their children must behave. Ana is allowed to date, but she must be home earlier than most of her friends, and her parents insist on always spending 15 minutes or so with any boy she's going out with for the first time. "We want to be sure you're doing the right thing," her mother explains. "There are so many bad ones out there, it's important to be sure."

Ana must also stop by the store each morning on her way to school to show her parents what she's wearing that day. When she was younger, they sometimes told her to put on a different blouse or to take off some of her makeup. "When you go out, you want people to see that you know how to conduct yourself," her father says. "You don't want to look like the kind of girl who would wear that—it needs to be washed!"

One important family time in Ana's house is Sunday dinner. Then the store is closed and everyone is together. Ana's mother makes a huge, wonderful meal and everyone sits around the table, eating, laughing, and joking. Ana always stuffs herself at this dinner. Then, in order not to gain weight, she tries to eat very little the next day.

Ana and her family are proud of her good grades. Ana has an older brother and an older sister who are now married, so it looks as though Ana may be the first person in her family to go to college. This fall term, senior year, is the last chance

Ana has to pull her grade-point average up even higher, and Ana works hard at her homework every night.

Then in the middle of the term, Ana's old history teacher gets sick and a new one takes her place. The new history teacher has a completely different way of teaching than the old one. He doesn't give tests with multiple choice and true-false questions. Instead, he gives essay tests and has lots of class discussion. He keeps telling the students that he wants to know what *they* think. When Ana asks if something will be on the test or wants to know what the right answer is, he laughs and says, "There is no right answer. What do you think?"

Ana is in a panic. She doesn't know how to get good grades from a teacher like this, and she worries that all her answers will be wrong. In fact, her midterm test comes back with a C-minus and a note that says, "All of this information is in the textbook. What is *your* opinion?" Ana studied even harder than usual for that test, and it scares her that the best she could do was a C-minus. She's willing to do anything to improve her grade, but she doesn't know what to do.

Ana gets more and more worried. She imagines getting her report card at the end of the term, with a big C-minus in history on it. Or maybe it won't even be a C, maybe her grade will go down to a D by then. She pictures how disappointed and upset her parents will be, and imagines how all her dreams of going to college are over. Ana feels like her whole life is coming to an end, and she doesn't know what to do about it.

One night, after she's been studying for a while, she comes down to the kitchen for a snack. Suddenly, she finds herself eating everything she can find. It's as though she can't stop. When the binge is over, she does feel calmer, but she's also worried about gaining weight. Now she'll have to skip meals tomorrow, to make up for today.

Then Ana has an idea. If she could throw up everything she just ate, she wouldn't gain any weight. She feels proud of herself for thinking of this solution to her problem. She eats a raw egg to make herself throw up, and when it works, she feels better than she has for weeks, like all the bad feelings have gotten out of her. She goes to bed feeling more relaxed than she has in a long time.

Ana promises herself that she'll never lose control like that again. But as the weeks go on and the situation in school doesn't improve, the anxiety returns. And Ana knows that if she does lose control, she can always make up for it by throwing up.

Cindy is excited about turning 16 because it means that she can finally take an after-school part-time job. Cindy wants to be a photographer and the local photo shop is hiring. The only catch is, she needs permission from her parents.

Cindy's father's favorite phrase is, "We'll allow you all the freedom you want—when you can handle it." When Cindy tells her parents that she wants to take the job, her father spends an hour with her going over her entire schedule. When will she study? When will she fit in her work on the school paper, which she needs to look good on her college application? When will she have time to practice her flute? When will she have time to spend with her friends—after all, it's important to be popular. Will her boyfriend mind that she is busier than usual?

Cindy has an answer for everything, so her father gives her permission. He tells her he's proud of her for being so well-organized and good at so many things.

As usual, Cindy's mother is skeptical. She doesn't think Cindy should take on an extra project—she won't be able to handle it. "If you have to take this job, at least give up one of your other activities," she says. Cindy sometimes feels like whatever she does, her mother won't like it. She's determined to prove that her father is right to be proud of her and that her mother is wrong to be concerned.

Gradually, though, Cindy starts to feel that she's not doing very well. She really doesn't have time to practice her flute enough. She thought she had gotten away with it by practicing extra hard the day before a lesson, but her music teacher finally said something to her. A few times she has been late to work because a meeting of the school paper ran late. She stayed late at work to make up for it, hoping that her boss really wouldn't mind, and so far he hasn't said anything, so maybe she has gotten away with that. But last week her math teacher made a little joke about her not being able to answer questions in geometry class, and Cindy wonders if he's realized that she's been studying less.

Cindy has always dieted very rigidly. Although she's never been fat or anywhere close to it, she'll skip two or three meals if the scale goes up even half a pound. Now, with everything else being so difficult, she notices that she's gained two whole pounds. She starts to panic, a panic that increases even more when her boyfriend makes a chance remark about her weight. He's only joking, but it scares her. She wants him to be proud of dating her, not ashamed to be seen with a fat girl.

Cindy starts to take laxatives to get the food out of her body. They don't really seem to help, but they do make her feel thinner. At the same time, she thinks about food more and more. She wishes she could eat, but she knows she can't.

One day, Cindy is in the school bathroom when she hears someone throwing up. Her friend Lisa comes out of the stall. She's surprised to see Cindy there, but explains that she throws up after every meal in order to keep her weight down. Cindy is thrilled. Finally, a solution to her problem! Finally, she can eat everything she wants and get away with it!

At first, Cindy is happy about having a solution to her problem. Gradually, though, she begins to feel disgusted with herself. The throwing up smells bad, and her throat is often sore. It's hard finding places to vomit where she won't be noticed, and she worries that someone will catch on. What scares her most of all is that when she tells herself to stop, she can't. Somehow, whenever she gets nervous, she finds herself eating huge amounts of food, and then she just can't stand herself until she gets rid of what she's eaten.

Tisha is only 15, but sometimes she feels like the grownup around her family. Tisha's parents are always worried about something, and it's usually Tisha who has to reassure them. Her parents are proud of their independent, successful daughter. "You do things we could never do at your age," her mother tells her. "You know more about what you're doing than I do," her father says whenever Tisha comes home with a new idea.

Tisha's boyfriend also admires his smart, attractive girlfriend. He is always asking her advice about problems with his family, with school, and on his job. Tisha usually has a good suggestion for him, and enjoys it when he brags about her to his friends.

Tisha's girlfriends also come to her for help with their boyfriend problems. They all think Tisha's boyfriend and her relationship with him are great, and they admire her for that.

The one thing Tisha isn't happy with is her weight. No matter how much she tries, she always seems to find herself eating an extra dessert or a second helping. Tisha is on the track team, so she can usually get in some extra exercise to make up for the eating. But she feels like she's always worried about when the food will catch up with her.

The summer she's 15, Tisha goes away to be a counselor at a summer camp. She's the first one in her neighborhood to do something like this, but she read about the camp, wrote away for information, and got the job. Everyone thinks it's just like Tisha to go off on an adventure.

But once Tisha gets to the camp, she finds it a difficult experience. The other counselors are all from the same school, so she feels left out. It's hard work taking care of little children, and Tisha isn't always good at it. She misses her friends, her boyfriend, and her family, but she doesn't want to let on that she's homesick because she knows they're all expecting her to have a great time at camp.

Worst of all, her weight is going up and up and up. There's no track at camp, of course, so she can't run off the extra pounds the way she's used to. And in her lonely, nervous state, Tisha is eating more and more.

Tisha starts to panic. The other counselors already think she's different—if she gets fat, they'll really look down on her. She imagines the kids making fun of her, too. She has to do something about this! But she can't seem to stop eating.

One night, in desperation, Tisha goes to the bathroom and makes herself throw up. She feels a little bit of relief that at least she won't gain any weight that day, but she also feels disgusted with herself. But somehow she has the sinking feeling that she isn't going to be able to stop eating or to stop throwing up afterward.

Ana, Cindy, and Tisha each have different stories, but they all have several things in common. They are all very worried about their images, how they present themselves to the world. They are also all quite concerned with pleasing others. Although each comes from an apparently loving family, each family has a problem that it has not admitted, being more concerned with preserving the appearance of a happy family.

Ana has learned that in her family, other needs must always come before her own. Her parents' need to run their store is always more important than anything she needs, and she is supposed to accept this and to go along with it, putting the store first the way her parents do.

Of course, economic necessity often does make demands on families. But Ana has gotten the message that her parents consider her needs a bother because they interfere with more important matters. By expecting Ana not to bother them "unless it's very important," Ana's parents have trained her to think of herself as a burden. And they've trained her to think that she's not allowed to have problems of her own, or to expect help and support when things are difficult.

With their careful attention to Ana's clothes and boyfriend, Ana's parents have given her another message: not to trust her own judgment. Since her parents are constantly reviewing Ana's decisions, Ana feels that her own judgment must not be very good. She decides that it's more important to please other people than to please herself.

The one time Ana feels that she can freely accept love and support from her family without worrying about being a burden is when she's eating. The family's Sunday dinners are times when there is enough love, time, and attention to go around. So Ana eats everything she can get, as though she were storing up her family's love.

That helps explain why Ana turns to food when she feels troubled. Because she can't go directly to her parents for support, eating feels like a way of getting support indirectly.

Because Ana has been taught not to rely on her own judgment and not to seek help from others, she's in a real bind when confronted with a new problem. She has only an old solution—eating.

Ana has been given a lot of messages about not admitting or expressing her "bad" feelings. She's not supposed to be angry that her parents are busy with the store, she's supposed to be understanding. She's not supposed to want independence or the chance to make her own mistakes, she's supposed to be happy to accept her parents' opinions. In a sense, Ana's bingeing and purging is her attempt to get the things she needs—love, comfort, support—while "getting rid of the" feelings she's not supposed to have. Because Ana's needs and feelings are very powerful, she needs to express them somehow. If she can't find a way to do it more directly, she may not be able to get off the binge-purge cycle.

Cindy's parents put a lot of effort into seeming happy and successful, and they expect their daughter to do the same. They, too, are nervous about allowing their daughter to make her own decisions. And like Ana, Cindy feels that there's no room for her to try things out or to make mistakes.

Cindy also has feelings that she feels bad about and tries not to have. Deep down inside, she's angry that she always has to prove herself to her father, and she's angry that her mother never seems to be pleased, no matter what Cindy does. She's also angry that she is supposed to consider their opinions about their activities first and put her own opinions second.

On the other hand, Cindy is so used to letting others make her judgments for her that she lets her life get out of hand. Although she herself knows that she can't handle all the activities she has taken on, she waits for her limits to catch up with her. It's as though nothing she does counts until someone else mentions it. That's the way Cindy has found for trying to have a little independence from her parents without really seeming to—if they don't notice she's doing something on her own, it doesn't count.

Even though she's unconsciously angry about trying to please others, it makes Cindy very nervous when she can't do it. Because her parents have put such emphasis on pleasing them, Cindy worries that if she can't please a person, she won't have any love or attention at all. Anything that's not pleasing—wishes for independence or extra weight—must be carefully hidden away.

In this context, Cindy turns to food as her secret, the thing that she can have to please herself. But because she can't let anyone know she has pleased herself, she's afraid that the food will show in the form of extra weight.

At first, Cindy would starve herself in order to keep up appearances. Now, purging seems like another way to "get away" with pleasing herself while seeming to give all her attention to others. One problem remains, however: Cindy still feels out of control. Because she hasn't really resolved her conflict between pleasing others and pleasing herself, she still feels anxious and worried. Only now her worries focus on food, instead of on the real issues.

Like Cindy and Ana, Tisha has grown up thinking that other people's needs were more important than her own. Her insecure parents needed her to be strong, so even though Tisha was just a child and they were adults, she took on a grown-up role before she was ready, in order to make them feel better.

Tisha has learned that she gets lots of rewards for taking on this role. Her parents praise her, her boyfriend depends on her, her friends admire her. The only problem is, sometimes she needs some of that love and support that she gives to everyone else—and who is going to give it to her? Tisha has learned that it's her job never to admit that she needs help but always to reassure others. So when she needs some love and support, she tries to give it to herself—through food.

When Tisha is in a new situation, the old pressures are still there, but not the old rewards. At camp, Tisha still feels the pressure to be strong and competent, but she's in a new situation and does need help. No one is telling her how much they admire her for being strong, so Tisha panics and turns to another old reward—food.

But Tisha feels that if she gains weight, that's the same as admitting that she's out of control, needy, and helpless. Because those are the problems that made her panic in the first place, they increase her panic even more. Even though Tisha is disgusted by the idea of throwing up after she eats, she is willing to do it because keeping control and hiding her needy feelings are more important to her than anything else.

The irony for all three girls is that bingeing and purging create more problems than they solve. Although Ana may feel calmer after a binge-purge night, she hasn't really figured out what to do about her history teacher, and she's even more afraid to ask for help than before. Cindy hasn't really solved the problem of which activities are most important to her and how to organize her time, and she's created a new problem, a new secret that she has to hide. Tisha's bingeing and purging don't help her to fit in at camp, and in fact will isolate her even more as she spends more time looking for food and for places to purge herself.

The good news for all three girls is that there is another solution. If they can learn to face the feelings that are being expressed through food, they can make life choices that are much more satisfying. Ana might learn that her needs are not burdensome and that her judgment is very good, when she pays attention to it. Cindy might realize that her life works better when she is looking to herself for information about what she can and can't do, rather than waiting for her mistakes to catch up to her. Tisha might be able to accept that sometimes she needs help and support as much as anybody else and find ways of getting it when she needs it. All three can go on to resolve their relationships to food and to the other issues in their lives.

6

What Can I Do About It?: Getting Help

The first step to getting help with an eating disorder, either your own or someone else's, is to recognize that a problem exists. As we've said, in this culture, almost everyone has some difficulties relating to food and weight, so it's not always easy to recognize a genuine disorder. If you think that you or someone you know has an eating disorder, we urge you to look back over the checklists in the earlier chapters to see if you notice any of the warning signs mentioned. We also urge you to pay attention to your feelings—a sense of discomfort or repeated thoughts of an incident or person might be your way of trying to tell yourself that your sense a problem.

As we've said, there are no hard and fast definitions that clearly divide all people with eating disorders from everyone else. In general, if an eating pattern has come to be the basis of all or most of a person's decisions, if it has become an obsession; or if it has become the focus of a great deal of time and energy, it is probably an eating disorder, particularly if the pattern lasts more than a few weeks.

If you do suspect an eating disorder, we urge you to act on your feelings quickly. The sooner that someone intervenes, the better the chance of resolving the disorder and the medical problems it has created. The longer an eating disorder persists as a way of coping with anxiety, anger, or other feelings, the harder it is to give up—and the more severe the medical consequences will be.

Why It May Be Hard to Accept Help

Later in this chapter, we'll talk about the kinds of help that are available for people with eating disorders, their families, and their friends. First, though, let's take a quick look at why it may be difficult for someone with an eating disorder to admit that she has a problem and to be willing to accept help.

As we've seen, many people with eating disorders are preoccupied with their appearance and with the opinions of others. The eating disorder may have developed in the first place because of a wish to appear thin and attractive, or to appear to be strong and in control. If a person believes that she has no right to her own needs, that her angry or frightened feelings are ugly, or that others are continually waiting to judge her, she will have a very difficult time admitting that she's human and needs help like everybody else.

Furthermore, as we've seen, people with eating disorders frequently come from families where parents are very concerned with maintaining control. In such families, when parents seem to offer help, they are really asserting their own power over their children. Alexis's mother's "help" with her daughter's clothes and makeup, for example, was a way of signalling Alexis that her mother was better than she was because, as an older woman, she knew more about how to be attractive. Cindy's father's "help" with his daughter's schedule was his way of telling her that he didn't trust her own judgment about what she could and couldn't handle.

If a person has developed an eating disorder out of frustration with this situation—in order to develop some kind of privacy and independence—naturally it will be difficult to accept the help of a counselor, therapist, or support group. It may seem that everyone who offers help is actually trying to run that person's life, to get her to do things their way, or to prove their superiority.

Many of the parents we've looked at also gave the message that they were afraid to have their children make mistakes or experience difficulties. Ana's parents, for example, were so frightened of Ana wearing the wrong clothes that they inspected her every morning. Kira's mother wouldn't even let her daughter speculate about possible problems in her ballet career. Again, eating disorders may include a daughter's fears of disappointing her parents or of overwhelming them with her own problems. These are the very feelings that make it hard to admit that they have run into something that they just can't handle—their relationship to food.

Another reason that it may be difficult for people with eating disorders to seek help is the widespread misinformation about what weight means. As we've seen, stereotypes and misunderstandings are especially prevalent about people who are overweight.

Compulsive eaters and the people who know them sometimes think of food, eating, or weight as the reason why other problems are occurring. Many people, for example, believe that being overweight is the reason that a girl isn't dating. Yet many girls who are overweight date actively, while many more conventionally attractive girls do not.

People may also assume that compulsive eating inevitably leads to certain problems: being lonely and isolated, for example. Thus if a girl like Maggie is clearly not lonely or isolated, her compulsive eating is dismissed or ignored. And if a girl like Charisse seems to be conventionally attractive as well as popular, it's easy to assume that she has no problem. These assumptions make it difficult for girls like Maggie and Charisse to seek the help they need or to be taken seriously when they ask for help.

Another stereotype about compulsive eating and being overweight is that the fat person's problems will all be solved as soon as she loses some weight. But the problems that arise from compulsive eating aren't necessarily solved when the compulsive eater diets successfully or manages to lose weight. We saw in Chapter 3 that many compulsive eaters have powerful reasons to remain heavy. Therefore, even if a heavy compulsive eater does somehow manage to control her weight through dieting, she hasn't necessarily solved her problem. She may become a compulsive dieter, like Charisse, or a bulimic, like Tisha. She may even become anorexic, like Leonie.

Often, people who are overweight assume that all their problems come from their physical appearance and that losing weight would leave no reason for anything other than total success. This assumption may be quite frightening, however. If the girl believes she's not capable of the success that she's "supposed" to have, she may not know how to face life without the excuse of her weight. If the girl has some reason for fearing success—such as Luisa, who fears that her parents will be jealous and angry if she dates—then she may be frightened of losing weight. Naturally, these fears make it difficult to seek help for a problem with compulsive eating.

Because a thin body is so tied up with images of glamour and success in our culture, there's a lot of pressure on teenage girls to be thin. If a girl has been taught to put her parent's needs first, and if her parents are unhappy or troubled about something, a girl may even wonder whether she deserves to be thin. How can she achieve this "success" when her parents are so unhappy?

These pressures are especially strong on girls whose mothers place a great deal of emphasis on their own looks. If a girl's mother views getting older as becoming more unattractive, she may give her daughter the message that her daughter doesn't deserve to be attractive while her mother cannot be. If the daughter believes she doesn't deserve to be attractive, and if she sees attractive and thin as the same thing, she may feel that she doesn't deserve to lose weight. Naturally, if she doesn't deserve to lose weight, she won't feel that she can seek help to do so, or to resolve her difficult feelings surrounding food and eating.

What about the girls who know that no matter what they do, they will never achieve the "perfect" body? Or the ones who know that they can achieve it only through starving themselves or abusing themselves with purging and extreme exercise? For these girls, the problem is not so much letting themselves lose weight as accepting the bodies they were born with and learning to find them attractive. But if a girl is too attached to her image of thinness and beauty, she may fear that getting help will mean giving up her chance of ever achieving that image.

Looked at in this way, eating disorders may seem like a vicious circle. The very forces that drive girls to unhealthy attitudes about bodies, food, and weight are the same forces that keep them from getting help in changing these attitudes. In fact, one powerful force that drives them to develop eating disorders is the feeling that they cannot or should not ask for help!

However, there is another side to the coin. The very fact that a girl has developed an eating disorder means that she has made her problem visible. She may have hidden her angry or anxious feelings before, but now she is gaining weight, losing weight, dieting compulsively, or bingeing and purging. She is doing something that she and others may notice and recognize as a sign that something is wrong. And this sign may be the first step on the road to seeking help.

A Word About Diets

As we've seen, many people with eating disorders think of diets, will power, and the control of their food intake as the solution to their problems. When they first seek help, they may do so in the form of turning to a diet center or diet group. Or they may go on diets with their friends or ask their friends or family to monitor their food.

In some cases, this may be effective. Sometimes, if a girl identifies to herself and others that she is not happy about her weight and her eating habits, and turns to others for support, she is acknowledging that she is a person with limits and a person who deserves love and support. This may be all she needs to solve her problem.

In the vast majority of cases, however, turning to diets will only make things worse. First, as we've seen, if a person has a powerful reason to gain weight or to binge, her willpower will be on the side of eating, not on the side of dieting, no matter how much she wishes it were otherwise.

Second, because diets are not addressing the real emotional problems behind the eating disorder, they are bound to fail. And to the person with the disorder, this failure is just one more proof that she is bad: out of control, too needy, too greedy, or just plain not deserving of anybody's help.

If a person binges or eats compulsively out of a feeling that she isn't getting enough of what she needs in her life, dieting will only feel like she is depriving herself further. Even if she succeeds on the diet, she will be unhappy about the deprivation. Even if the diet "works," she is likely to feel like a failure, because her problem was so big that even losing weight didn't solve it.

If a person like Luisa loses weight, she may still not have friends or a boyfriend if she doesn't also address the things in her situation that make it hard for her to reach out to people. If a person like Maggie loses weight, she will still feel insecure about her parent's love if she hasn't also looked at that issue and found a way to resolve it.

What we're saying is that diets work only for one thing—to lose weight—and they may not even work for that. The person who diets and doesn't lose weight, or who does lose weight but doesn't change her life, will be even more frustrated and unhappy than before. In general, diets aren't the solution to eating disorders. They may even create more problems.

When Someone You Know Needs Help

It's hard to watch someone you know endure an eating disorder. You feel bad for the person and want to be able to help. You may feel angry that the person is hurting herself in this way, and you may also feel angry that her behavior seems to be controlling you. You may feel guilty that you can't seem to help or inadequate because you don't know what to do. If your friend has sworn you to secrecy about, say, her binges or her purges, you may feel torn about your loyalties: you know she needs help but you don't feel right "telling" on her.

The first thing to remember about your situation is that *you* are not the one with the problem, so *you* are not the one who can solve it. There are some positive things you may be able to do to offer your friend or relative love and support or to help her to get the counseling or other treatment that she needs. But in the end, the decision to seek help must come from her, not from you. All you can do is be ready to help when she's ready to accept help.

If you know someone you're concerned about and you haven't talked about it with her, breaking the silence is the first step. Your main objective should be to let the person know that you know and that you care.

This may be a difficult encounter, so be prepared. Pick a time to speak when you both feel calm. Find a way to talk when you won't be interrupted. You might want to write down your feelings before you talk with your friend or relative, in order to get clear on exactly what you want to say. Writing about your worries, your feelings for her, and your hopes for her getting help might help you to sort through your feelings and get clear on what you want to tell her. You may also want to practice what you want to say with someone else or by yourself.

When you do speak, your friend may not want to have the conversation. You may need to say something like, "I know this is hard, but it's important to me to tell you how I feel about this," or, "I know it hurts to talk about it, but I really need to hear how you feel." Your focus should always be on talking about how you feel, not on what you think she should do or is doing.

It may help to start your sentences with *I*—"I care about you and I'm worried when I see you getting so thin," or "I see you gaining a lot of weight very quickly and I'm concerned that something is bothering you." However, just because a statement starts with *I* doesn't mean it's really about your feelings. Be careful of statements like "I don't understand how you can do this to yourself!" or "I don't think it's very healthy to throw up that way"—those statements sound more like negative judgments than like genuine expressions of concern.

If you feel that the conversation is getting out of control, find a way to end it. You don't have to take back what you've said, but you can agree that for a while, you won't talk about this again. You might say something like, "I'm sorry that you feel so upset, so we don't have to talk about this now." No matter how strongly you feel that your friend is hurting herself and needs help, it won't help either of you to get into a fight.

Be prepared for a lot of different reactions from your friend. She may be relieved that she doesn't have to keep her secret any longer. She may be furious and tell you to mind your own business. She may tell you that you're wrong and she has no problem or she may attack you, pointing out the things you have trouble with.

Try not to take any of her reactions personally. Keep telling yourself that this is her problem. Even if she is correct in saying something critical about you, that's not the issue, and her reasons for making the criticism have a lot more to do with her than with you. If you feel too upset to continue the conversation, find a way to end it. If she tells you you're wrong, but you still feel she has a problem, you may want to acknowledge that the two of you disagree while sticking to your own point—"I understand that you're not worried and that you think you can handle it, but I see you getting thinner and thinner and I am still very worried."

If the conversation goes well, you can go on to discuss how your friend or relative can get help. If the conversation goes badly, you can end the conversation. Then you have to decide what to do next.

If you think your friend is in trouble, we urge you to tell someone about it. Call a hotline or one of the organizations listed at the back of this book. Tell a counselor or tell another sympathetic adult whom you trust. Even if your friend has sworn you to secrecy, it's more important to get her help than to keep your promise. Many teens with eating disorders refuse to get help until parents force them into treatment. Often the most you can do for a friend is to tell her parents about the problem.

We also urge you to tell your friend what you intend to do. That way, you have been honest and clear about your actions. You're giving your friend the message that you care about her and that you trust her to handle the information about what you're going to do.

Of course, in an emergency, you should take action immediately. If your friend collapses, faints, or attempts suicide, be sure to tell a responsible adult whom you trust to take action.

Accepting Your Limits

It's very difficult to watch a friend or a family member struggle with a problem. It may help to keep reminding yourself that it's her problem and that you can best support her by letting it be her problem. Here are some do's and don'ts that may help you do that.

Don't:

... offer to go on a diet or eating plan with her. This may only make her feel like she has one more person to please.

... offer your advice about what food to eat when you go out with her. Let it be her decision how she eats.

... offer your opinions about how she looks, good or bad. If she asks you, say you have always cared about her and you feel bad when she puts looks above everything else. If she makes a positive statement about herself and asks you to agree, don't judge her looks, say something like, "I'm glad you're feeling good about yourself."

... try to guess what she wants or needs—ask her directly!

... try to be her therapist or feel like you have to have all the right answers—let her solve her own problems.

Do:

... stay in touch with her and continue to do social things together.

... make time to talk about *your* problems and concerns, not just hers.

... make your own food decisions, rather than feeling controlled by her food issues.

... get the support or counseling you may need from others, especially if you are dealing with a family member.

What Kinds of Help Are Available

Here is a look at the different kinds of help that might be useful for someone with an eating disorder. Some of the things on this list—such as work with a nutritionist or a support group—may work best along with counseling or some kind of family treatment. A person with an eating disorder may need many different kinds of help: changing her relationship to food, addressing the underlying emotional issues, and changing her relationship to her family. She may also need medical, dental, or gynecological treatment for problems that have arisen from her eating disorder.

What order these forms of help come in may vary. Keep in mind, as you read about the different types of help, that they are all available and may each be useful in its own way.

Telling a Friend

If an eating disorder has become an ugly secret, telling a friend may be the first step toward acknowledging a problem and getting more substantial help. Admitting your problem to a friend may make the problem seem more manageable. You will also find out that people will not necessarily look down on you for having problems—after all, everyone needs help sometimes.

Support Groups and Other Organizations

There are many organizations devoted to eating disorders and food issues. Some are listed in Chapter 7 of this book. You may find out about others through the yellow pages, your school counselor, or your local social-service agency.

Some of these groups offer only information. Others offer counseling. Still others offer support groups—groups of people who all share the same eating disorder, frequently led by an experienced counselor or person who once had the disorder but has recovered. These groups are a chance for a person to see that she is not alone with her problem and to learn new ways of thinking about both food and her other relationships.

Counseling

Counseling for eating disorders may be available through your school or through a local social-service agency. There are many different types of counselors. To find the type of counselor that is right for you, you may need to get help from an adult you trust. Be sure, though, that whichever counselor you choose, he or she has experience with eating disorders. Basically, what you can expect from a counselor is the chance to talk about your life with someone who is supportive, kind, and nonjudgmental. A counselor may help you to accept feelings that make you uncomfortable. He or she may help you gain new insights into things that have puzzled you or troubled you. Ideally, a counselor will help you both accept yourself as you are and go on to make the changes that you would like. She or he does this through listening, asking questions, and, occasionally, suggesting another way of viewing a situation that you may not have thought of.

Family Counseling

As we've seen, eating disorders may have their roots in family relationships. If the person with the eating disorder is still living at home, she and her family may benefit from counseling for all of them together or for each of them separately. A family counselor can help every member of the family express his or her frustrations and so help the entire family find better ways of dealing with their problems. Ideally, a family counselor helps every member of the family find a way of relating to the family that is more satisfying for all concerned.

Nutritionist

In addition to counseling and other support, a person with an eating disorder may also want to work with a nutritionist. A nutritionist can help identify food allergies, cravings, vitamin deficiencies, hypoglycemia, and other nutritional problems that may be contributing to eating disorders. She or he can help develop a diet that will feel satisfying while helping the person to gain or lose weight. She or he can also help anorexics and bulimics address the nutritional problems they may have created while dieting, fasting, or purging.

Hospitalization

The last resort for all those with eating disorders is hospitalization. Some anorexics must be hospitalized in order to be force-fed. People with other eating disorders may collapse from medical problems resulting from their eating patterns.

If a person has not chosen to seek help, hospitalization may feel like a betrayal. The anorexic who is not ready to eat may be especially angry at this intervention.

On the other hand, if hospitalization is a last resort, it also brings home to the person with the eating disorder that her disorder is threatening her life. Likewise, hospitalization makes her problem very clear to her family. In some cases, this is what it takes for them all to be willing to accept the help they need.

When Other Problems Are Involved

Sometimes a person with an eating disorder develops other problems as well, such as addictions to drugs or alcohol or a dependence on diet pills. In such cases, it's important to seek help for these problems as well.

Likewise, a person with an eating disorder may be facing family problems of drug or alcohol abuse, sexual abuse, or physical abuse. We urge people with these family problems to seek help, either through an organization or through an adult that they trust. More information on such organizations is available in Chapter 7 of this book.

Finding New Ways

Seeking help for an eating disorder may at first be a painful experience. The person realizes that she must give up an old way of coping before she has learned another way. She realizes that she can no longer keep up the facade of being perfect or completely in control, that she must face some feelings that she has been trying to avoid, and that she might have to accept some truths that at first appear unpleasant.

However, confronting old secrets can also be a powerful relief. Because she no longer has to pretend that everything is fine, the person is free to imagine new and more satisfying ways of living and relating to others. Because the old ways of coping clearly don't work, the person has the chance to find new ways that work better. Best of all, acknowledging an eating disorder and committing herself to overcoming it means that she can look forward to the day when food is no longer a terrifying temptation or a shameful secret, when it is just another enjoyable and satisfying part of life.

7

Where to Find Help

The following organizations offer a variety of services to those who suffer from eating disorders. They offer counseling referrals to anorexics, bulimics, compulsive eaters, and members of their families.

Eating Disorders

National Associations and Programs

American Anorexia/Bulimia Association, Inc. (AA/BA)
293 Central Park West
Suite 1R
New York, NY 10024
(212) 501-8351

Anorexia Nervosa and Related Eating Disorders, Inc. (ANRED)
P.O. Box 5102
Eugene, OR 97405
(541) 344-1144
http:// www.anred.com

National Eating Disorders Organization (NEDO)
6655 South Yale Avenue
Tulsa, OK 74136
(918) 481-4044

Local Programs

The following programs are run by hospitals to help those who suffer from eating disorders.

American Eating Disorders Center
330 West 58th Street
Suite 200
New York, NY 10019
Attn: Dr. Henry Grayson
(212) 582-5190

Anorexia/Bulimia Treatment and Education Center
The Edgewood Complex
St. John's Mercy Medical Center
615 South New Ballas Road
St. Louis, MO 63141
(314) 569-6898

Child Guidance Center of Children's Hospital of Philadelphia
34th Street and Civic Center Boulevard
Philadelphia, PA 19104
(215) 243-2600

Cleveland Clinic Foundation
Section of Child and Adolescent Psychiatry
9500 Euclid Avenue

Cleveland, OH 44195
(216) 444-5812

Eating and Weight Disorders Clinic
Johns Hopkins Medical Institutions
Meyer Building 101
600 North Wolfe Street
Baltimore, MD 21287
(410) 955-3863

Eating Disordered Program
Providence St. Vincent Medical Center
9205 Southwest Barnes Road
Portland, OR 97225
(503) 216-7080

Eating Disorders Clinic
Children's Hospital Medical Center
Department of Psychiatry
OSB-4
3333 Burnet Avenue
Cincinnati, OH 45229-3039
(513) 636-4737

Eating Disorders Clinic
Children's National Medical Center
111 Michigan Avenue NW
Washington, DC 20010
(202) 884-2164

Eating Disorders Clinic
Fairview University Medical Center
420 Delaware Street SE
Box 301 Mayo
Minneapolis, MN 55455
(612) 626-6188 (psychiatry clinic)

Eating Disorders Clinic
Lucille Salter Packard Children's Hospital at Stanford
725 Welch Road

Palo Alto, CA 94304
Attn: Tom McPherson
(415) 723-5467
(415) 497-8000 (general clinic)

Eating Disorders Program
Center for Addiction
Tennessee Christian Medical Center
500 Hospital Drive
Madison, TN 37115
(615) 865-0300, ext. 4800

Eating Disorders Program
Children's Hospital Medical Center
Department of Psychiatry
Fegan Building
8th Floor
300 Longwood Avenue
Boston, MA 02115
(617) 355-6728

Eating Disorders Program
Neuropsychiatric Institute
University of California at Los Angeles
760 Westwood Plaza
Los Angeles, CA 90024
(310) 825-0478

Eating Disorders Program
New York Hospital
Cornell University Medical Center, Westchester Division
21 Bloomingdale Road
White Plains, NY 10605
Attn: Dr. Gary Nichols
(914) 997-5936

Eating Disorders Program
Northwestern Medical Faculty Foundation
303 East Ohio
Suite 550

Chicago, IL 60611
(312) 908-1838

Eating Disorders Program
Porter Memorial Hospital
2525 South Downing Street
Denver, CO 80210-2944
(303) 778-5774

Eating Disorders Unit
Massachusetts General Hospital
15 Parkman Street
Boston, MA 02114
(617) 724-5600

Eating Disorder Treatment Center
150 Medical Way
Suite C-3
Riverdale, GA 30274
Attn: Dr. Rush
(770) 996-4264

Canadian Programs

Adolescent Clinic
Montreal Children's Hospital
1040 Atwater
Montreal, Quebec
Canada H3Z 1X3
(514) 934-4481

Eating Disorder Program
Ward 7A
Toronto Hospital for Sick Children
555 University Avenue
Toronto, Ontario
Canada M5G 1X8
Attn: Heather Brown, Intake Coordinator
(416) 813-7195

Eating Disorders Program
B.C.'s Children's Hospital
4480 Oak Street
Vancouver, British Columbia
Canada V6H 3V4
(604) 875-2200

The following organizations offer a variety of services to those who suffer from problems that sometimes face those with eating disorders.

Alcohol and Drug Problems

Al-Anon Family Group Headquarters
200 Park Avenue South, Room 814
New York, NY 10003
(212) 254-7230
(212) 260-0407

See the white pages in your telephone book for the group in your area. Al-Anon helps those over the age of eight deal with problems created by alcoholism in friends or family members.

Alcoholics Anonymous World Services
475 Riverside Drive
New York, NY 10115
(212) 870-3400

Provides free referrals for those seeking recovery from alcohol problems.

Narcotics Anonymous World Service Office
19737 Nordhoff Place
Chatsworth, CA 91311
(818) 773-9999

Provides general reference services for those seeking recovery from narcotics addiction.

The National Helplines
American Council for Drug Education
164 West 74th Street
New York, NY 10023
(800) 435-7111

Provides information on specific drugs and treatment options and referrals to treatment programs, self-help groups, family support groups, and crisis centers nationwide.

Pills Anonymous
P.O. Box 248
New York, NY 10028-0003
(212) 874-0700

Self-help group for individuals with pill dependency problems.

Physical and Sexual Abuse

Children's Aid Society
33 Charles Street East
Toronto, Ontario
Canada M4Y 1R9
(416) 924-4646

Kempe National Center for the Prevention and
  Treatment of Child Abuse and Neglect
1205 Oneida Street
Denver, CO 80220-2944
(303) 321-3963

Provides individual and group therapy for children who have been victims of child abuse. Also provides consultations to professionals who work with children.

National Clearinghouse on Child Abuse and Neglect
  Information (a division of The National Center on Child
  Abuse and Neglect/Children's Bureau—NCCAN)
P.O. Box 1182

Washington, DC 20013-1182
(800) 394-3366
(703) 385-7565

Provides information and referrals through a DIALOG database.

New York Society for the Prevention of Cruelty to Children
161 William Street
12th Floor
New York, NY 10038
(212) 233-5500

Provides referrals and counseling to families and children suffering from physical and sexual abuse.

Saskatoon Society for Protection of Children—Crisis Nursery
1020 Victoria Avenue
Saskatoon, Saskatchewan
Canada S7N 0Z8
(306) 242-2433

VOICES (Victims of Incest Can Emerge Survivors) in Action, Inc.
(773) 327-1500

Provides help for people who have been sexually abused by family members. Volunteers will give referrals to self-help groups, therapists, and agencies in their communities.

For Further Reading

The following books will provide further information on eating disorders.

Kolodny, Nancy J. *When Food's a Foe: How to Confront & Conquer Eating Disorders.* New York: Little, Brown, 1992.

Kubersky, Rachel. *Everything You Need to Know about Eating Disorders.* New York: Rosen Publishing Group, 1995.

Matthews, John R. *Library in a Book: Eating Disorders.* New York: Facts On File, 1990.

Moe, Barbara. *Coping with Eating Disorders.* New York: Rosen Publishing Group, 1995.

Nardo, Don. *Eating Disorders.* San Diego: Lucent Books, 1991.

Sirimarco, Elizabeth. *Eating Disorders.* Tarrytown, New York: Marshall Cavendish, 1993.

Sonder, Ben. *Eating Disorders: When Food Turns Against You.* New York: Franklin Watts, 1993.

INDEX

A

Abraham, Suzanne 48, 79–80, 82
Abuse—*See Physical abuse; Sexual abuse*
Adolescents—*See Teenagers*
Advertising
  images of thinness in 1–2
Age
  anorexia nervosa by 59
  bulimia by 75
Alcohol abuse
  blood sugar and 21–22
  bulimia and 82
  compulsive eating and 31
  organizations for 117
  in parents 13
  weight gain and 24
Allergies
  compulsive eating and 32
  food 107
Amenorrhea 51
  anorexia nervosa and 10, 16
Anger
  appetite and 12–14
  feelings of 5
Anorexia nervosa 47–71
  bingeing and 49–50
  bulimia and 74, 79–80
  case studies 64–71
    dancer (Kira) 64–65, 69
    parental pressures (Alexis) 65–67, 70–71
    sexual abuse (Leonie) 68–70
  cessation of menstruation and 10, 16
  compulsive eating and 52
  families and 60–64
    father 60
    "model child" 61–62
    mother 60–61
    parental needs 62–63
  by gender 5
  medical effects 56–59
    long-term consequences 59
    physical symptoms 57–58
  parental pressure and 8, 10
  prevalence 59–60
  recognizing 50–56
    dieting and weight loss 53–54
    eating rituals 54–55
    excessive exercise 55
  secretiveness and withdrawal 50–51
  telltale signs 51–52
  "starving away" of adult sexuality and 16–17
Anorexics 47–48

Appearance, physical
  anorexia and 61
  bulimia and 83
  teenage girls and 12–13, 15
Appetite
  anger and 12–14

B

Bingeing 33–34
  by anorexics 49–50
  definition 3, 33
  in non-bulimics 74
  obesity and 80
  secrecy of 8
Binge-purge cycle
  control and 77–78
  as "solution" 83
Biological factors
  compulsive eating 28–32
    addictions 30
    allergies 31
    blood sugar 28–29
    nutritional deficiencies 29–30
  weight 23–25
    calorie theory 23
    set-point theory 24–25
Blood pressure
  obesity and 36
Blood sugar
  fasting in bulimics and 80–81
  and feelings of hunger 28–29
  regulation of 20–22
Body image
  ideal female 64–65
Body size
  rebellion and 9–10
Boys
  eating disorders in 6
Bruises
  in anorexics 57
"Bulimarexics" 79–80
Bulimia 72–95
  anorexia nervosa and 74, 79–80
  case studies 85–95
    lack of independence (Cindy) 89–90, 92–95
    parental needs (Ana) 85–88, 91–92, 94–95
    parental pressure to act as "adult" (Tisha) 90–91, 93–95
  definition 3
  families and 82–85
    emphasis on appearance 83

father 85
mixed messages 82–83
mother 84–85
by gender 5
incest and 17
medical effects 80–81
in men 78
parental pressure and 8, 10–11
prevalence 81–82
progression 76–80
  anorexia and 79–80
  obsession with food 78–79
  purging 77–78
recognizing 76
sexuality and 16–17

C

Caffeine
  addiction to sugar and 31
  blood sugar and 21–22
Calorie theory 23
Carbohydrates 21
Carpenter, Karen 65
Case studies
  anorexia nervosa 64–71
  bulimia 85–95
  compulsive eating 37–46
Children—*See also Teenagers*
  of weak parents 13–14
Chocolate
  addiction to 31
Circulation, blood
  obesity and 36
Compulsive eating 27–46
  anorexia nervosa and 52
  biological factors 28–32
    addictions 31
    allergies 32
    blood-sugar level 28–31
    hypoglycemia 29–30
    nutritional deficiencies 30–31
  case studies 37–46
    family expectations (Charisse) 40–41, 44–45
    loss of control of relationship with parents (Maggie) 39–40, 43–44
    suppression of anger (Luisa) 37–39, 41–43
  definition 3, 33
  by gender 5
  medical effects of 36–37
  prevalence of 35–36
  recognizing 32–35
    compulsive dieting 34
    lack of pleasure from food 33–34
    telltale signs 35
    weight loss as "solution" to 99
Counseling 106–107
Crash, blood-sugar 22–23
  in hypoglycemics 30–31
Cravings 30–32, 107

D

Davis, William 82
Dehydration
  in anorexics 57
Depression
  anorexia nervosa and 57
Diabetes
  hypoglycemia and 29
  obesity and 36
Diabetics 21–22
Dieting—*See also Weight loss*
  by anorexics 53
  compulsive eating and 34
  preoccupation with 3
  shortcomings of 100–102
Diuretics 52
Drug abuse
  blood sugar and 21
  bulimia and 82
  in parents 13

E

Electrolyte imbalances
  bulimia and 81
Equilibrium, weight 24–25
Esophagus, ulcerated 81
Exercise
  anorexia nervosa and 55
  bulimia in men and 78

F

Family—*See also Parents*
  anorexia nervosa and 8, 60–64
  bulimia and 8, 10–11, 82–85
  demands on daughters from 9–10
  difficulty with teenage transition 7–8
  help from 6–7
  metabolism rates and 23–24
  mixed messages from 15
  single-parent 9
  unspoken rules in 11–13
Family counseling 107
Fasting
  in bulimics 80–81
Fat
  female sexual development and 48–49
  as "protection" 16–17
  role of liver in metabolizing 24–25
  and self-image in anorexia 58–59
Father
  of bulimics 85
  in families of anorexics 60
  physical changes in daughter and 15–16
Feelings—*See also Anger*
  anorexia nervosa and suppression of 63
  bulimic binges as escape from 78
  eating disorders and 6
  sexual 7
  weak parents and repression of 13–14
Flour—*See Processed flour*
Fonda, Jane 65
Food
  allergies 107

anorexia nervosa and obsession with 54–56
bulimia and obsession with 78–79
compulsive eating and lack of pleasure from 33–34
preoccupation with 3
sexuality and 14–17

G

Gender
 anorexia nervosa by 59
 compulsive eating by 35–36
 eating disorders by 5
Girls—*See also Teenagers*
 anger and 5
 mixed messages given to 1–2
Glucose 80
Growth spurt
 in teenage girls 48
Guilt
 compulsive eating and 33

H

Heart problems
 bulimia and 81
 obesity and 36
Help 96–109
 availability of 18–19
 counseling 106–107
 diets as inadequate 100–102
 difficulty in accepting 97–100
 family counseling 107
 finding new ways of 108–109
 for friends 102–104
 hospitalization 108
 limits to 104–105
 nutritionist 107
 for other problems 108
 support groups 106
Hospitalization 58–59, 108
Hunger
 anorexics and 56
 coming to terms with 25–26
 theories of 20–23
Hypoglycemia 29–31, 107
Hypothalamus
 hunger and 20–21

I

Ideal woman 2
Incest 17
Independence, desire for 7–8
Insulin 21–22
Intestinal failure
 in anorexia nervosa 59
Ipecac 81

K

Kidney failure
 in anorexics 57

L

Laxatives
 anorexia nervosa and 59
 bulimics and 77–78
Liver
 damage to in bulimia 80
 metabolic role of 24–25
Llewellyn-Jones, Derek 48, 79–80, 82

M

Magazines
 images of thinness in 1–2
 for men 5
Malnutrition 24
Maturation 7
Medical effects
 anorexia nervosa 56–59
 bulimia 80–81
 compulsive eating 36–37
Men
 bulimia in 78
 eating disorders in 5
 magazines for 5
Menstruation 7
 anorexia nervosa and cessation of 10, 16, 51
Metabolism 20–21
 theories of 23–25
 weight and 23–24
Mineral deficiencies 30–31
Miss America 2
Mixed messages
 bulimics and 10–11, 82–83
 from family 10–11, 15
 in relationships with boys 15
 from society 1–2
Monroe, Marilyn 2
Mother
 of bulimic girls 84–85
 competition from 15
 in families of anorexics 60–61

N

Nicotine
 blood sugar and 21
Nutritional deficiencies 30–31
Nutritionists 107

O

Obesity
 bingeing and 80
 compulsive eating and 34
 definition 5, 36, 48
 psychological problems associated with 37

P

Pancreas 21–22
Parents
 of bulimics 83–85
 drug or alcohol problem in 13

help from 6–7
need for reassurance from children 13
teenage changes and 7–8
teenagers expected to behave like 9
Playboy (magazine) 2
Prevalence
anorexia nervosa 59–60
bulimia 81–82
compulsive eating 35–36
Processed flour
addiction to 31
Puberty, female
development of fatty tissue and 48–49
Purging
definition 3
"discovery" of 77
secrecy of 8

R

Rebellion
eating disorders as type of 9–10
Responsibilities
eating disorders as protection from 9
Rituals, eating
anorexics 54–55
bulimics 79
Rules, unspoken
in family 11–13

S

Secrecy 8
compulsive eating and 35
Selfishness
fear of 13
Self-protection
eating disorders and 14
Set-point theory 24–25
Seventeen (magazine) 2
Sex—*See Gender*
Sexual abuse 17
Sexuality
anorexia nervosa and female 10
conflicts about and food 14–17
Single-parent families 9
Starchy foods—*See Carbohydrates*
Stereotypes 98–99
Sugar, blood—*see Blood sugar*
Sugar, processed
addiction to 31
Suicide 14
Support groups 106
Sweets
blood sugar and 21–22

T

Teenagers
anger in 12–13
anorexia nervosa and 63–64
changes in 6–7
eating disorders and 5–6
hormonal changes in 49
as "parents" 9
sensitivity to appearance in 12–13
Television
images of thinness on 1–2
Thinness
anorexia nervosa and social preoccupation with 48
media images of 1–2
pressure on teenage girls for 99–100
social desirability of 1–2
Tooth decay 81

U

Ulcerated esophagus—*See Esophagus, ulcerated*
Unspoken rules
in family 11–13

V

Vomiting
bulimics and 78

W

Weight
biology of 23–25
coming to terms with 25–26
compulsive eating and 34
misinformation on significance of 98
preoccupation with 3
as sign of emotional conflict 37
variances from ideal 47
Weight gain
bulimics and fear of 79
set-point theory of 24–25
Weight loss—*See also Dieting*
family failure to recognize 8
and sense of control in anorexia nervosa 53
as "solution" to compulsive eating 99
Willpower
compulsive eating and 4
diets and 101
Withdrawal
anorexia nervosa and 50–51

Paula F. Hadley Memorial Library
Boston High

616.85
Mal

C2

DATE DUE		

Paula F. Hadley Memorial Library
Boston High